# NOTES TO AN ACTOR

# NOTES TO
# AN ACTOR

## RON MARASCO

*Ivan R. Dee*

CHICAGO    2007

www.ivanrdee.com

Library of Congress Cataloging-in-Publication Data:
Marasco, Ron.
    Notes to an actor / Ron Marasco.
      p. cm.
    Includes bibliographical references and index.
    ISBN-13: 978-1-56663-757-2 (cloth : alk. paper)
    ISBN-10: 1-56663-757-0 (cloth : alk. paper)
  1. Acting. I. Title. PN2061.M2277 2007
792.02'8—dc22

                      2007011653

*for E.C.M.*

# CONTENTS

# NOTES TO AN ACTOR

# INTRODUCTION

# "Do you have any notes for me?"

If you are an actor, or have spent any time around actors, this question probably has a familiar ring.

"Do you have any notes for me?" is something actors always ask because, strangely enough, they actually *like* getting "notes" on their work. They have come to depend on whatever little nuggets of insight or inspiration they can use to make a performance better. So they *welcome* notes—more than welcome them, they *demand* them.

After a show, actors have been known to hold friends hostage in a bar till dawn looking for notes. Or, if a director skips over them during the post-rehearsal "note session," there's a good chance an actor will be waiting for the director in the parking lot to plead for a note.

Of course, sometimes "Do you have any notes for me?" is really actor code for, "Do you have any *compliments* for me?" But most of the time actors really mean

3

it. They want a *note*: a useable piece of advice—some kind of talisman against failure which they can carry into the night.

This desire for notes is mostly an "actor" thing; people in other fields tend not to have it. Painters don't ask for notes, nor do stockbrokers or teachers, and it's also hard to imagine a football player in the pub, after a game, saying, "Hey fellas, got any notes for me?" (Writers will sometimes ask for notes, but if you give them any they'll disagree with everything you say and never talk to you again.)

So, why are actors first among professionals in their need for notes?

I think it has to do with the nature of acting itself. Acting is such a mysterious art. It can't be learned in a nice, neat, logical, step-by-step way—like computer programming or chess or fencing or even singing. You learn to act as you learn to live or love: through experience, by trial and error, by succeeding and failing.

An actor develops by (what James Joyce called) *epiphanies*: those quick moments of insight and "dam-breakage" that come as a gift and hit you at odd times. Like when you're driving or showering, or (best of all) during a live performance, when something strange and new opens up in you and you're suddenly playing a moment better than you ever thought you could.

Over time, a handful of these moments of insight soak their way into your brain and become your technique.

These insights, these epiphanies, are what I call "notes." I have always believed that all good actors have them etched in an imaginary notebook in their minds, and I thought it would be helpful to put one into book form for actors. Thus: *Notes to an Actor*.

When the best-selling novelist Elmore Leonard was asked the secret to his writing, he said, "I leave out the parts that people skip." That's what I've tried to do in this book. I've left out the parts that I know actors will skip. (Actors are notorious skippers!) There aren't a lot of long explanations, there's no specialized acting terminology, and (thank God!) no detailed descriptions of acting exercises.

It's just the essentials, just notes on acting. All of which have been gathered over a long period of time and filtered through the perspective of actors whom I have known and taught.

I have always asked the actors in my classes to give me a copy of the notes they took throughout a course. Over time, I noticed that there were a few things I said that almost every actor always seemed to write down verbatim—often with underlines and exclamation points. *Notes to an Actor* is a collection of these "keepers."

Once this book gets started, it consists only of notes. So, let me explain the point of each chapter up front.

Chapter One gives notes on what I call *Perspective*. The actress Ruth Gordon once said, "It's not enough to have talent; you have to have *talent for having talent*." We've all known good actors whose talent or whose careers were hurt because of something screwy in their *perspective,* either on their acting or on themselves.

Your *perspective* is the soil into which you plant the seeds of your talent. If the soil is bad, you're in trouble.

The notes in this chapter are meant to help you develop this healthy soil, or a "talent for having talent."

Chapter Two is about the characteristics of pure acting *Talent*. It could, of course, be called *talents*—plural, because there is such a variety of attributes and approaches that can be used to act, just as there are many different kinds of actors, all the way from a die-hard theater pro who's done all the classics to a model-turned-starlet who thinks Chekhov is a kind of vodka. These notes are about how to develop the talents that the actors I love and respect seem to have.

Chapter Three is on *Rehearsal*. Too often I've seen actors give a better performance in the first table-reading of a play than they did on opening night, because of a rehearsal process that paralyzed them. This chapter is about how to rehearse with something in mind they tell doctors in the Hippocratic Oath, which is: "First, *do no harm*!"

Chapter Four is about giving an actual *Performance*. These notes are about how to stand "out there" in the rough weather of really *doing* it. How to confront the hazard, mystery, and difficulty of "delivering the goods" in performance.

Chapter Five is about what I call *Greatness*. We all know that a *great* actor is very different from a *bad* actor, but I have come to believe that a *great* actor is also very different from a merely *good* actor. The *great* actor does certain extra "things," and the notes in this chapter are about those special things. This chapter is for actors who are hovering between *good* and *great* and looking for the final push.

The notes in these first chapters give practical advice about being a skilled actor in general. The notes in the next three chapters are about how to apply those skills to some of the different kinds of acting you may be called upon to do: comedy, Shakespeare, and acting for either stage or film. While these last chapters are no less practical than the first ones, they also look at any "theoretical" aspects of these genres that I think contains secrets for how you can play them better.

Chapter Six is on *Comedy*. But it's not just for comedians; it's for any actor who has to play comedy, even if it's just a comic moment in a serious show. There's that famous old story that theater folks always tell about an actor on his deathbed who was asked what it was like to die. Supposedly he said, "Dying is easy. *Comedy* is hard." I've never actually heard anyone explain exactly *why* comedy is so hard. This chapter looks at what is hard about comedy, in the hope of making it a little easier for actors to play it.

Chapter Seven is about *Shakespeare*. While this may seem odd to include in such a small book on acting, I've found that the same skills you need to do Shakespeare will help you play many other kinds of special material: anything that has heightened speech and style, from plays with complex language that are set in a specific time period to "historical" movies like *Gosford Park* or even *Lord of the Rings*.

The final chapter is called *Stage and Screen*. Most good actors regularly move between *film and TV* work and *theater* work. They love theater because the roles are bigger and deeper, and because they get to "live" as the character for longer chunks of time without some-one yelling "Cut!" They love film and TV for both economic and artistic reasons. This last chapter is about how to move back and forth between these two hemispheres of the good working actor's world.

So there you have it. A small book of notes to an actor. You can read the chapters beginning to end, or "jump around" (which is how most actors like to read). I hope the book will be inspirational. At times I know it will be *blunt*, but I have never met a good actor who didn't prefer harsh honesty to polite evasion.

Think of this book as a "note session." Each chapter gives a handful of quoted "notes"—the kind an actor might jot down on the back of a script. Each note is then followed by a short riff on it—the kind a director might give. Finally, at the end of each chapter you will find a summary of those notes in list form.

Whenever you pick up this book, imagine the two of us sitting in an empty theater after rehearsal, drinking lukewarm coffee, smoking cigarettes, and talking the night away. Which is, after all, the way it's really done.

CHAPTER ONE

# PERSPECTIVE

*Always aim for the creative state*

The actor's life is a bizarre one, filled with all kinds of contradictions and diffusions. One minute you're pouring your heart out in a scene, the next minute you're pondering the merits of a new hair color; one minute you're on stage playing *Medea*, the next minute you're auditioning for a fabric-softener commercial. It's hard to know how to focus your efforts. Consequently actors can get sidetracked and feel artistically lost. They lose perspective on their acting, and on the nature and purpose of acting in general.

To prevent that from happening you need to keep your overall *goal* in mind. And what do I mean by a goal? Just as in sports—it's when you score, win, get it just right. So let's start from the actor's winning moment and work backward. Here is the actress

Colleen Dewhurst's description of what happens when your acting is "on."

> The great moment on stage is when suddenly, out of nowhere, a flush comes over you—and you're flying! You're not even walking anymore, you're soaring. And nothing you can do is wrong. And you know it. The actor you're with knows it. And the best thing is you can touch each other and both begin to soar and everything closes out, and the scene is the same, but something different is happening between you.

It's not just actors who have this kind of great moment. People in other fields know the feeling just as well. Athletes call it being "in the zone." Jazz musicians call it being "in the pocket." Gamblers call it "luck." Religious people call it "grace."

The great acting theorist Stanislavski called it the "creative state." It's when inspiration hits you, and a force that is greater than yourself seems to take the wheel from you and propels you to a higher level of work.

You don't get to the creative state by trying, or by "pushing," or even by studying. You get to it by becoming more honest in your work and in yourself. There is a line in an Arthur Miller play in which a character says, *"Every man has his star. The star of his honesty. You spend your life groping for it. But if it goes out it's gone for good."*

The whole aim of your work as an actor should be to follow the star of your honesty. Because more often than not it will take you in the direction of the creative state.

## Try to lose yourself

*"Losing through you what seemed myself,*
*I find selves unimaginably mine."*—e.e. cummings

Whatever the creative state is, it's the opposite of ego-driven self-consciousness. In fact the "creative state" usually comes when you care more about someone or something else that's on stage with you than you do about your own performance. Whenever actors talk about experiencing this state they almost always say it feels like they were "losing themselves." Here's how Matthew Broderick described it:

> There can be moments on stage—but sometimes in a movie, too—where you just feel you're in a golden space. You're in this strange world where everything you do makes sense. And it's funny, the audience is right with you, and the other actors, and you get these rare moments of feeling at one with something. You hear voices in your head. Do I sound like Joan of Arc? It's like you're not in a play anymore. You're saying the words, but *you're not watching yourself. You know, you spend most of your time on stage, or at least I do, watching and criticizing your performance.* But every now and then it's a great feeling.

This loss of *self-consciousness* is a difficult thing to achieve because so much of what you're called upon to do in acting ramps up self-consciousness. I mean, could there be a more self-conscious situation on earth than being up in front of an acting class filled with scrutinizing actors; or being at a final callback in front of a

roomful of producers who can either hire you on a series (for twenty thousand dollars per episode) or send
you back to your job at Starbucks?

But *hyper-self-consciousness is death to acting*.
Think about it. When you mess up as an actor—blow an
audition, say—it's usually because you were too self-
conscious and tried too hard. Actors never do well when
they spend days on end working with their acting coach,
their acupuncturist, their shrink, and the local Wiccan
in preparation for the big audition. They go into those
auditions looking like a desperate actor and don't get
the part.

But time and again you hear of actors who *do* get the
big part when the final callback happened on the day
their car got towed, or their cat had a seizure, or their
head cold was so bad that the only thing they cared
about during the audition was not blowing a snot bubble. The reason actors do well in such cases is because
these petty "problems" make the actor stop thinking
about himself or herself. And while the brain is looking
away from your "performance" for a few seconds, that's
often the time the creative state sneaks in and takes
over the controls.

Of course, most actors have fairly sizable egos, so
the idea of being able to set the self aside is not easy.
But the fact is, you only need to do it while you are actually acting. Actors can care about only themselves all
day long (and many good ones do) so long as, when the
moment comes for them to begin acting they let that self
go and lose themselves to the character.

One obvious example of the needy "self" at the actor's core of most actors was Sally Field's famous "You

like me, you really like me!" Oscar acceptance speech. (Famous, probably, because she *said* in public what most actors *feel* in private.) But there's another story about Sally Field that, to me, shows her ability to control that "need to be liked" *at the moment she starts actually acting.*

In the movie *Norma Rae* (for which she won her first Oscar) there is a scene in which her character—a feisty union organizer—is pulled out of a factory and shoved into a police car by the cops from her hick town. The director told Field that her character would fight as hard as she could to keep these two beefy redneck cops from getting her into the squad car. When they did the scene, Field—who probably weighs ninety pounds—fought so hard she ended up hurting the huge actors who played the cops, and actually broke one guy's rib.

This actress may be desperate for people to like her all day long, but at the moment she becomes a character and enters into a scene, she loses that "self" and all its ego needs and is able to fight like a hero for what her character wants.

## Have a shit detector for too much acting

Ernest Hemingway said "the most essential gift for a writer is *a built-in, shockproof shit detector.*" I think every actor should have a shit detector too—an inner warning system that lets you know when you're bad. And in acting, *bad* means you look like you're acting.

Ask anyone to do an imitation of a *bad* actor and they'll show you a kind of acting that *calls attention to the acting.* They'll put on a showy voice, make grand gestures, and be full of over-the-top emotions—all de-liberately obvious acting-with-a-capital-A. One of the strange truths of acting is that you are good at it in di-rect proportion to "how little you seem to be doing it." No one says to a dancer after a show, "You were great! I couldn't even tell you were dancing!" But the good ac-tor should never lean toward "acting."

When Burt Reynolds was an up-and-coming film ac-tor, he met Spencer Tracy, an actor legendary for the believability of his work. When Tracy asked, "What do you do, young man?" Reynolds said, "I act." To which Tracy replied, "Well, don't let 'em catch you at it."

*Don't let 'em catch you at it.* Now that's a shit detec-tor.

Ironically, *acting* is the enemy of acting. It's actually better to do nothing at all than to do too much. I once did an experiment in which I videotaped an actor. I told him to look down at a table as if it were a loved one lying on a slab in the morgue. He did his usual forced self-indulgence. I wanted him to do something unself-consciously, even if it meant doing something very sim-ple and almost meaningless. I pulled him aside and said, "Now, just go up and look at all the little chips in the paint that are on the surface of the table." I asked the next class to look at the two "takes" and told them that both of them were of a man looking at a loved one in the morgue. I asked them to tell me which of the two takes was best. It was unanimous: the second take.

*Don't let 'em catch you at it.*

Cut out the acting. If you're running lines for a scene with another actor and a friend walks up and says, "Hey guys, what *scene* are you rehearsing?" you may need to oil your shit detector. If on the other hand, the person comes up and says, "Hey what are you guys arguing about, I thought you were friends?!" it means your shit detector is in good working order.

Finally, be aware that calling attention to one's acting happens a lot more often than most actors realize. Even very good actors will sometimes slip under the radar of their shit detector and fall into look-at-me-act acting. It's a lifelong struggle.

Stanislavski told a story about one such actor, who couldn't stop himself from "acting," even to the very end!

> I happened to be present at the deathbed of one actor. He seemed to be acting even in that moment. Even in delirium. Even in the throes of death, his facial muscles went on habitually acting the part of someone dying.

Thus the lot of an actor—getting an acting note even on his deathbed.

## Don't show—know

The reason why actors need to have shit detectors is because audiences have them!

Audiences can sense—if only on a subliminal level—when an actor is or isn't being truthful. All human beings have a mechanism for sensing the truth about others. It's wired into us as a species, which makes sense because as useful evolutionary endowments go, the ability to sort out true from false is a pretty handy survival skill.

Of course, our ability to sense truth becomes clouded when it's something subjective. (Your friends always know that the person you are dating is a jerk long before you see it.) But take any average human being, and ask him or her to sense the truth about something or someone. If they have an entirely unbiased opinion and can be objective, most people will be amazingly good at sensing what is and isn't true. And this includes audiences.

The most common form of "lying" to an audience is when actors try to manipulate them, when an actor does something in front of an audience for *the effect* it will have on an audience rather than by experiencing the moment themselves as the character. I call this kind of acting "*showing* rather than *knowing*."

I once saw a scene in an acting class that began with the character waiting for a bus. The actor playing the role kept looking anxiously in the direction from which the imaginary bus was expected. Then he glanced down at his wrist as if checking the time on a watch. But since the actor didn't have a watch on, and since the teacher (like all sensible people) hated miming, the scene was stopped. She told the actor not to "indicate" to the audience by pretending to look at a nonexistent watch. The teacher then asked another guy in the class to lend the actor doing the scene his watch to use and had the actor start the scene again. This time he looked down at the watch and looked back impatiently toward where the bus was expected.

Again the scene was stopped by the director. She asked the guy, "What time is it?" There was a pause, and then his sheepish face told the tale. Even though he had a real watch to look at, he didn't *really look at it*. He was still in a mode of showing things to the audience rather than experiencing them himself.

It's the smoking gun of all manipulative acting.

## Truth is bigger than "the personal"

While a commitment to being "truthful" in your acting is a good thing, don't be one of those actors who believe so deeply that they must *completely* feel the truth of what their character is feeling that they become indulgent about it.

There are actors whose "sense of truth" has a narcissistic bent to it. In rehearsal these actors make everyone wait while they go through showy versions of suffering for their art—tears in the dressing room long after the scene is over, and so forth. On stage this can manifest itself in indulgent acting that makes you want to put up a sign that (in the words of the playwright Paul Rudnick) says: "Road closed. Man acting."

On a deeper level, don't automatically equate *truth* with your own *personal* reality. Some truths are more profound than your own personal truth, and plays and movies tend to be about these bigger truths. Don't always use your limited experiences as touchstones for what is and isn't true. A lot of times you hear American actors say about a certain moment in a scene, "This doesn't feel comfortable to me." It's hard to imagine a Kabuki actor, clad in his hundred-pound costume and headdress, saying something like that.

Until your life is interesting enough to have someone write a play or movie about it, assume that the truth of the play is more profound than your own personal experience. Rather than take great dramatic material and shrink it down to fit into your own scope, try instead to *extend* yourself into the larger truths that good material gives you the opportunity to experience.

There is a passage from the notebook of the writer Alfred Kazin that I sometimes suggest an actor write on a piece of paper and put in his or her wallet:

> I pray to get beyond myself, to indicate to this believing unbeliever that there is a territory beyond this bundle tied up so angrily in the night. I pray to be relieved of so much "self." I ask to be extended.

## Don't overidentify with one acting method

There are often two types of people in acting classes. The first is the person who thinks that the teacher is brilliant, feels that he or she is continuously having acting "breakthroughs," and loves talking about these breakthroughs up in front of the class. The second type thinks (often correctly) that the teacher dislikes them. They feel the class hasn't changed their acting very much at all, and they hate it when other actors get up in front of the class and talk about their breakthroughs.

It has been my experience that the *second type* of actor is usually much better than the first.

It's a universal acting law: the person whose love of acting is equal to his love of poker is usually a better actor than the person whose license plate says 4ACTING.

Actors who, in the first few minutes of knowing you, feel obliged to tell you they are "Meisner trained" or "so-and-so trained," would, believe it or not, make someone like Sanford Meisner cringe. None of the great acting teachers would want you to serve some acting procedure rather than have the acting procedure serve you. In fact, Sanford Meisner kept a sign over his desk that said, "There is no right or wrong, only true and not true."

While many great actors did study with people like Meisner or Stella Adler or Uta Hagen, good actors don't limit themselves to the strict dos and don'ts of any one dogma. Real acting talent needs more elbow room than that.

Your acting methodology shouldn't be used as a way of projecting an "identity" to the world. Actors who do this tend to care more about the *process* of acting than the eventual *result* of it. This tendency can be because the results of their acting have not been so hot, so they become "purists" in order to give themselves the ego boost one normally gets from getting work.

Another type of person who identifies too strongly with one acting method is someone who has a weak sense of his or her own identity as a person, and so they try to fill the void with a group identity that is centered on a doctrine.

When it comes to acting books, read them to get what you can out of them, and read the ones that address specific problems you have as an actor. If, for example, you can tap into emotion easily but find that you get stuck in your own small self and *don't expand into the world of the play*, read Stella Adler's *The Technique of Acting*. If you play characters well and can jump right into the world of the play but *don't make enough of a personal, emotional connection to your work*, read Lee

Strasberg's *A Dream of Passion* or Bobby Lewis's *Method or Madness*. If you give "impressive" but selfish performances and *don't relate well with other actors*, read Sanford Meisner's *On Acting*. If you're too cerebral and *can't let yourself be physically and imaginatively free*, read the work of Michael Chekhov or Moshe Feldenkrais or books on the Alexander Technique. If you have trouble *behaving in a believable way* on stage or on a set, read Uta Hagen's *Respect for Acting*. Finally, for *pure inspiration* about acting, the best book I know is *The Mystic in the Theatre* by Eva Le Galliene, about the actress Eleonora Duse. It's the most sensible book I know about the spiritual aspect of acting.

Above all, remember: any acting class or acting book that makes you enjoy acting less should be cut out of your life. Most people become actors because they not only liked it when they were first exposed to it (usually starring in a school play), but it also made them feel more powerful. As the learning process kicks in, however, both the joy and the power can dry up, often because of well-meaning but ineffectual teachers, directors, and acting books.

Remember: *the energy that comes from enjoying what you do and the power it fills you with may be more useful, ultimately, than any acquired techniques.*

### Avoid the drama-around-the-drama

Actors are drawn to the dramatic. It's nothing to apologize about. In fact, it's an asset. Since it's an actor's job to experience situations and feelings that most people normally would want to avoid, a little benign addiction to drama is actually useful and is, for sure, a very common trait in actors.

But sometimes the pull toward drama can turn into a syndrome that I call "the drama around the drama." This is when all kinds of offstage turmoil creates more drama around the *doing* of a show or movie than there is in the performance itself.

Some common dramas-around-the-drama are: intercast romances, director-versus-actor power struggles, actor-to-actor personality clashes, wars between cliques, people with "attitudes," people with attitudes about the people with attitudes, and, finally, a difficult actor's readiness to dump a truckload of emotional baggage onto an entire cast.

Good actors know that they have only so many megabytes of emotional energy. They use them on stage, where it counts, and don't waste them on offstage dramas. But inferior actors actually use the drama-around-the-drama as a way of compensating for the limits of their talent. They don't have the talent to do it on stage, so they do it offstage where you don't need talent to get attention. Haven't you ever noticed that the guy who has the worst complaints and the best gossip always plays Spear Carrier No. 3, while the talented leads tend to be more docile backstage? Haven't you noticed that the person who gets the most attention at the cast party is rarely the person who is able to get that much attention on stage by virtue of his or her acting?

One final point on this. Actors always vehemently agree with me about the "drama around the drama." They can cite dozens of actors who are guilty of it. Yet I've never once heard an actor admit that *he* or *she* does it. It's easy to fall into, and it is one of the actor's most dangerous pitfalls.

## Keep auditions confidential and in perspective

The single most important healthy perspective for an actor to have is a good attitude toward auditions. Nothing can shatter your focus as an actor and "set you back" the way an unsuccessful audition can. Just about all actors have had one big role they lost, the mere mention of which can, even years later, cause the same stab of pain as the memory of a lost love.

The auditioning process will always be painful, but there are things you can do to protect yourself from its power to devastate you. For one thing *never tell anybody (who does not absolutely have to know) about your big auditions*. Agents: yes, they will know anyway. Cabdrivers who are driving you to them and who you will never see again: fine. Spouses: maybe. Parents and friends: never! Acquaintances: never, ever!

Some actors can't help but be tempted to tell people about their auditions, especially the "big" ones. They do this because just being able to report to loved ones and acquaintances that they are auditioning for "so-and-so-big-shot" or are up for "such-and-such-great role" can make them feel like they almost have the role already. It gives them a kind of Walter-Mitty, pipe-dream ego boost.

Chances are, when you have one of those big auditions, you won't be able to resist talking about it either, "Just this once." You'll tell actor friends to make them jealous. You'll tell relatives to reward them for their belief in you since you starred in school plays. You'll tell other miscellaneous people like your dentist, café cashiers that you make small talk with, and neighbors you bump into while taking in the mail.

The problem with blabbing about your audition is that, if you *don't* get the part, you'll not only have to deal with *that* disappointment, you'll also have to take yourself down a peg with your friends and endure the patronizing of well-meaning relatives—to say nothing of changing dentists, avoiding certain cafés, and retrieving your mail at strange times so you don't run into the neighbor who is "dying to know if you got the part!" For God's sake, do yourself a favor and avoid this potential horror.

Two final things to remember about auditions and maintaining a healthy perspective toward them. First, in general, *believability is more important than emotion*. Producers, especially in film and TV, are looking for someone who seems as if he or she is a real person. In an actor's zeal to *feel* in the audition, it's easy to push for a high level of emotion but end up coming across as over the top and unbelievable. No producer will fail to give you a role because you didn't ball your eyes out in the audition; but they won't give you a role if, in your quest to be emotional, you come off as histrionic.

Second, if you don't get a role, don't concoct a lot of hypothetical reasons why you didn't. A lot of actors come up with all kinds of dire interpretations of what happened in an audition. "They hated me!" Wait to hear it from a direct source. Unless your agent tells you, "Mr. Spielberg just called to say you were awful," don't assume the worst and create a lot of foolish hypotheticals to torture yourself with.

Most of the time, when you don't get a role it's not because your acting was bad. More likely it's because they wanted some quality you didn't have as much of as someone else did. So don't start losing perspective on "who you are" just because you don't get one role. There are simply some roles that you will not be the best person for, even though you had your heart set on getting them. That doesn't mean you aren't a good actor.

To make an analogy, if I were holding auditions for an Italian antipasto salad and into the audition room walked a batch of strawberries, even if they are the greatest strawberries in the history of agriculture, I wouldn't be able to use them for what I'm casting. And wouldn't it be ridiculous if one of these excellent strawberries said to itself, "Hey, I didn't get cast in the antipasto project, so maybe from now on I need to be more of a pimiento."

## Use who you are

Both in acting and in life, we are drawn to people who are *comfortable with themselves*, just as we feel subconsciously repelled by people who aren't comfortable with themselves. The writer Simone Weil once described the quality that "beautiful women" have; I think her observation can be applied to *all* actors. Weil said that the beautiful woman seems to say, *"This I am,"* whereas the ugly woman seems to say, *"This I am not."*

All *good actors* have a quality that says, *"This I am."* Inferior actors have a quality that says, *"This I am not."*

It is better to be comfortable with who you are, with all your idiosyncrasies and individuality, than try to project a false form of yourself to the world. Haven't you ever had this happen?—someone shows you a copy of their 8 × 10 in which they look far more glamorous than themselves, to the point where you almost want to say, "Great picture. Who is it?"

Trying to be someone you're not can often make you look less appealing than you are as your real, raw self. Being comfortable with who you are tends to be a very *attractive* quality. Laurence Olivier said that the goal of a great actor is that "every member of the audience— male and female—should want to sleep with you." No one wants to be with someone (in bed or otherwise) who doesn't seem to want to be with himself! Such people have a quality that seems to say, "I have something hidden and awful at my core, which you'll find out about if you get any closer." It's an aura that can be sensed by others—even audiences—and stops them from getting closer.

Finally, using acting as a way to present a certain image of yourself is antithetical to what acting is and, as Geraldine Page explains, can actually take the joy out of it:

> The reason acting is so painful for some people is because the reason they want to act is to convey to people something they aren't. In other words, they want to idealize themselves and have people see who they want to be. And they suffer a great deal when people don't respond to what they are trying to do. Whereas if you realize who you are and that your characters are your characters then you're free to do them.

## Don't fear downtime

One of the difficult things about being an actor is downtime. Not only do actors have a lot more time between jobs than people in other fields, but acting isn't a skill that can be practiced by oneself. A painter can sketch alone, a musician can play alone, even a basketball player can shoot baskets in the driveway. But an actor alone in a room doing a monologue to the mirror is a pitiful sight.

Many actors find downtime painful, which is a shame because downtime can be very healthy for your acting. Acting is the one art that people actually get *better* at by *not* doing it for a time. When you're away from it, your brain can gather new stimuli because it's freer to wander. As my grandmother used to say, "A watched pot never boils." When you have a little time off from acting you stop "watching" your actor-self; so, then, when you do get back to acting after a hiatus, you will often find a lot of nice surprises boiling up out of your unconscious.

And when you do have downtime, don't think about acting. Use it as an opportunity to leave that imaginary world that you probably spend too much time in and reconnect with the real world. Remember the characters that you play are people, not actors, something it's easy to forget when you are always working. Here is a little piece of a poem called, "Sentry Duty," by Tomas Transtromer. I think it could just as easily be called "prayer of the actor during downtime."

Task: to be where I am.
Even when I am in this solemn and absurd role:

I am still in the place where creation does some
work on itself.

Your creativity is always doing "some work on itself,"
especially if you leave it alone for a while.

## *Make the world*

The great pieces of theater and film live in the mind as
a complete *world,* a realm unto itself that has its own
population and norms, its own tone and spirit and culture. This is true of everything from great interpretations of classic plays such as Peter Brook's famous
circus production of *A Midsummer Night's Dream* to
movies such as *Young Frankenstein* or *Lord of the
Rings.* Either because of a good director, or maybe just
luck, great productions work because every actor in it
"gets it," every actor understands "the world" of the
show and finds his or her particular character's place
within that world.

As an actor you should focus on trying to weave this
"world-making" magic in every production you do.
You'll know you have done your job well if, years after
the project is over, you still think of it as if it were a
"world," a place you would revisit if you could.

Unfortunately there is a lot about the nature of acting and an actor's working life that will undercut your
ability to keep the character you play enveloped in this
imaginative world. There are forces that keep isolating
characters from the life-giving context they come from.

First there is the audition process. It's not unusual
for a working actor to go for months on end acting only

from "sides," those two to three pages of audition material that have been isolated from the full story of the character. Even if an actor can read the whole script—and in many cases that's not possible—he or she will tend to focus on the scene in isolation, and will develop only a "scene's worth" of the character's life, out of context of the overall emotional development the character goes through in the story as a whole.

If you are one of those actors who continuously hears that you gave a great audition but find that you don't end up getting the part ("You definitely gave the best reading, but the producers decided to go with someone else."), chances are you are giving a great performance of *a scene*—but may not fit into the larger world of the character. *That's* what producers have in mind when they cast—"the world" they are trying to produce. If this is the case with you, do a better job of considering the script as a whole and the character within that world.

Another aspect of acting life that severs a character from that world is scene-study classes. Too often actors work only on *scenes* in isolation from the larger play. There's an exchange in David Mamet's play *Edmond* in which a girl tells a guy that she is an actress. When the guy asks, "What plays have you done?" She says, "I haven't done any plays. Just *scenes*." Sadly, that's not far from the truth. Spend too much time on "scene study" and you can start to think of acting as a series of attempts "to get a scene right," rather than as immersion in a larger fictional world. And I would venture to say that most actors who do scenes in scene-study class haven't read the plays from which they were taken—

because they simply neglected to do so or because they "found the scene in a *scene book.*"

Given all of the above, you have to work hard not to sever your characters from the world that gives them real, organic life. What can help are certain kinds of improvisations. I am not in favor of typical "improvs" because I think they have a way of turning into "party games," in which people try to be more clever than believable. But some kinds of improvisations can be a useful way to explore "the world" your character lives in.

And I do think that improvs are a great thing to do alone or with only a few (serious) actors whom you trust. Flesh out the world of the play by imagining and doing little scenes that you think the text of the play may hint at but not fully explore. Improvs can teach you how much you have been depending upon the lines for your sense of the world, rather than trying to understand the fictional world your character is supposed to live in. They will also give you the feeling of spontaneity and unfolding mystery that should be the feeling you work toward in written and rehearsed scenes. You know you are starting to hit your stride as an actor when a rehearsed scene feels like it's being improvised. Improvisations rooted in truth, pushed beyond the notion of an acting exercise, are a good thing to try.

There is a story about the famous acting couple Alfred Lunt and Lynn Fontanne's legendary production of Chekhov's *The Seagull*. In one scene the characters are supposed to be offstage having dinner, which the audience is supposed to hear in the background, while another scene is going on on stage. Each night when they did the show the Lunts and other cast members actually *had dinner* offstage in the wings, in character. On stage you could faintly hear the table chatter and glasses clinking, all of which sounded very real—because it was! And to me it sounds like a fun thing to do. Talk about making the *world*.

---

## Summary of Notes on Perspective

1. *Always aim for the creative state.*
2. *Try to lose yourself.*
3. *Have a shit detector for too much acting.*
4. *Don't show—know.*
5. *Truth is bigger "than the personal."*
6. *Don't overidentify with one acting method.*
7. *Avoid the drama-around-the-drama.*
8. *Keep auditions confidential and in perspective.*
9. *Use who you are.*
10. *Don't fear downtime.*
11. *Make the world.*

---

CHAPTER TWO

# TALENT

## *Talent begins in sensitivity*

There is an assumption that actors are sensitive. The stereotype is that every actor absolutely brims with feeling, which may explain why it's always the kid who has the tantrums who gets earmarked early on as the "dramatic" one in the family. It has been my experience that the reverse is true, that actors are not necessarily people who are filled with feelings. Actors are people who *want to be* filled with feelings. Deep down, something inside most actors believes that they *don't feel enough*, and they become actors as a way of searching for more sensitivity.

Most talents, regardless of what they are, tend to originate from some kind of *sensitivity*. A painter's eyes, a surgeon's hands, even the fingertips of a baseball pitcher have extra-sensitivity. They say that the great jazz pianist Art Tatum had such a good ear that he could tell the difference between a penny and a dime dropped on a table.

The emotional sensitivity an actor needs is something that takes an effort to cultivate, but it also takes a clear understanding of how sensitivity actually works. Actors can't get it by reading *Sensitivity for Dummies*. Marlon Brando once said in an interview that "a sensitive person *receives fifty impressions* where somebody else only gets seven."

This is, I think, a very important secret to acting. A lot of actors think that being sensitive means going "inward" into themselves. But Brando—arguably one of the best actors ever—says *No*: to be sensitive you have to *receive* impressions, meaning they come from outside of you. In this big and interesting world, trying to find sensitivity by looking "inward" is like being in a restaurant and trying to find food within yourself.

Here's an example. Vanessa Redgrave was on a film set preparing to do an emotional scene. She asked the director if she could have a few moments of quiet before he called "Action." The director asked for it, and the set went silent. Redgrave lay there for a few seconds with her eyes closed, then suddenly looked up and said, "I'm sorry, but is there music playing somewhere?"

A lighting assistant, standing clear across the soundstage from her, was listening to soft music on a Discman—something he always did to block out the noise of a set while he did his work. He thought to himself, "She can't mean me." He figured there was no way she could hear music escaping from his tiny earphone from so far away, but just to be sure, he clicked his Discman off. Immediately Redgrave said, "Ah, much better. Thank you." And she went back to preparing for the scene.

The point of the story is not that Vanessa Redgrave has good hearing. It's that when a great actress is getting ready to do a demanding scene, she *does not close herself off* and go into her little mental world. Instead she *opens herself up* to her environment in order to feel the subtlest and most delicate physical energies in the space around her.

## *Acting is mixing molecules*

Sensitivity has a purely physical aspect. A lot of delicate work is required to make your self more sensitive in a modern world that hits us with such a barrage of sensory stimuli, often too much for a human body to process. Just imagine if someone from another era— Shakespeare's day, say—time-traveled to our world. Just think how he would react if he had the average American moviegoing experience at the local multiplex: the attack of lights and laser-generated effects exploding across the screen, the sound system that rumbles up from every inch of the room, the popcorn covered with an ocean's worth of salt, the sodas that always seem to have the word "burst" in their name, and the day-glo covered candy that is so sweet if you keep it in your hand for too long your palm gets a cavity. Face it—one of our normal days could kill someone from the 1500s.

Modern American sensory overload is something actors have to work hard to combat. Just like someone with overworked hands, our overworked sensory apparatus has become callused. The actor must try to open up and re-sensitize this callus. Kafka once said that a book "should take an ax to the frozen lake inside you." Good acting training should "take an ax to the frozen lake" that surrounds an actor's body, to try to open the actor up.

Try this experiment. Wherever you are right now, stop what you are doing and listen to the sounds around you. Try to identify at least *six* sounds. Do it now.

Chances are, you heard *something you hadn't known was there before*—the buzz of a reading lamp, a far-off air conditioner. You're opening up, re-sensitizing. You're melting Kafka's frozen lake. And this is an exercise you can do almost anywhere, anytime.

When you begin to open up your shell, it will make you better able to feel the subtle energies that come from other actors on stage with you. Glenn Close described acting as "a mixing of molecules." It's a great way to think about it. Because that's what happens between people in their most emotional moments, in both acting and in life. When people communicate emotionally, the invisible protective shield that we keep around us involuntarily opens up, and we feel another person in a way that registers in our skin, on virtually a *molecular* level. We say, "He makes my skin crawl," or we get "goose bumps," or we "tingle" or "flush" or become "pale as a sheet."

Great moments of acting happen when different actors' molecules mix. Thus the term, they had "good chemistry" on stage. Where there's no mixing, there's no chemistry. And you can mix only if you are exposed enough to allow the exchange.

Again, the American actor has even more to fight against in this regard. Our puritanical roots have made Americans overly aware and slightly alarmed about relating physically to other people. The person who stands too close to us in line at the bank is clearly a stalker; the friend who hugs too long is obviously coming on to us; the person next to you on the plane is violating your half of the armrest. By these prissy American standards, the entire country of Italy could be brought up on charges of sexual harassment!

But one of the major characteristics of talent, any talent, is a willingness to be *open*, to let some molecules out, to let some in.

## Try to tap your unconscious

The unconscious is the part of the mind from which all real creativity emerges. Like the famous story about the author Proust: one minute you're in a garden in France eating a cookie, the next minute a book starts bubbling up out of your brain, and ten years later you've written *Remembrance of Things Past,* all seven volumes of it. That was one hell of a cookie.

But that's how the unconscious works—some small, random image opens a door to a whole inner realm in your mind, and it's from that place of unsorted feeling and strange personal imagery that most creativity springs.

Here is a good, quick exercise you can do to practice tapping into your unconscious. Take a few minutes to try to recall a place you once knew very well but haven't seen in years. Somewhere like your grammar school, or a grandparent's summer home—that sort of place. Try to remember everything you can about it, and keep at it until you hit some detail that *surprises* you, something you literally have not thought about since you were there, a long time ago—something completely forgotten until now.

That springing of trapped imagery, that sudden rush of retrieved feelings is an opening into your unconscious.

This is a doorway that talented people—from writers to actors to architects to chefs—knock at frequently in the course of their work. In fact, a case could be made that it is the ability to tap one's unconscious that kicks a person's "skill" up to a level of *artistry*. The person who has skill but who can't tap his or her unconscious usually ends up being a technician as opposed to an "artist."

Those who can feed their skill with the resources of their unconscious can often make the people who see their work tap into their *own* unconscious. This is particularly true for actors and their audiences. As the brilliant Russian theater director Vahtangov said:

> Whatever is created *unconsciously* is accompanied. by a discharge of energy that has an affecting quality. This ability, the unconscious carrying away of the audience, is the characteristic of acting talent. Whoever perceives unconsciously and unconsciously expresses it—that one is a genius!

It's one of those strange "laws of creativity"—when you go to a deeper place in your mind, you can touch a deeper place in the minds of other people. Actors spend hours working on various acting skills but don't always give enough attention to trying to access their unconscious. It really is the magic door.

## Acting is tricking your brain

Acting is the only talent I know of that can be done at a "genius level" by anyone at all.

Let me explain. Imagine the following. I set up a mean trick to play on a woman who works as a checker in a supermarket. I bribe a policeman to walk into the store and tell the woman that her husband has just been killed in a car accident. The cop enters, conveys the awful news, and the woman "loses it," becomes hysterical.

Now imagine if, all along, I had a hidden camera set up that filmed the whole thing, and I take that footage and show it to an acting class, prefacing it by saying, "This is a small scene from an independent film I'm directing called *The Checker*, and it stars a woman from my acting class."

If I asked the class what they thought of the checker's "performance," is there any question what they'd say? Brilliant! Genius! A master of her craft! Because *everyone* has the ability to act. All you have to do is make happen to yourself what happened to this checker: *trick the brain*, create belief for yourself.

The best way to trick your brain is simply by pretending. This may be the essence of acting talent: the ability to pretend.

People too often use the word "pretend" to mean either "lying" or "playing," neither of which does the word justice. The word "pretend" actually comes from the same root as the words "tendon" and "extend," so the word in its origin was all about "stretching." And that's a good way to think about it. When you pretend, you aren't being untrue, you're just *stretching your truth* into the circumstances of the character.

*You trick your brain not by lying to it but by stretching it.*

Practice little exercises of tricking your brain. Pretend, for example, when you are driving home from acting class that you are on your way to hear "the big jury verdict" that will determine your guilt or innocence. Or pretend when you're trying to fall asleep in bed that you are Juliet in the tomb and you just took the apothecary's drug. Or try this one: stare at your phone and try to believe it is ringing and that it's the murderous stalker calling again. Stare and stare at the phone and pretend. When one day you're doing this and the phone *rings*, imagine the shot of adrenaline that will be released from your "tricked" brain!

Then, some wonderful night on a stage or on a movie location, you'll be doing a scene and all of a sudden you'll successfully trick your brain into believing what the character believes. You'll get a jolt. And you'll see just how profound pretending can be.

## The more talented actor hits more notes

The term "notes," in this instance, is not the kind I have been referring to throughout this book. In this case I mean *musical notes,* like a pianist strikes on a keyboard. A talented pianist, one who is a virtuoso, is able to "hit more notes," with more specificity, in a shorter period of time than the nonvirtuoso.

In the case of the virtuoso actor, the notes are not the individual sounds struck on a keyboard. The actor's "notes" are those small shifts in behavior—the tiny changes that go on in the actor's thoughts, body, and perceptions as he or she acts. What it takes to be a virtuoso in acting is the same as what it takes to be one in music: you have to be able to *hit more notes, with more specificity, in a shorter period of time* than the nonvirtuoso actor.

Here's the way a *good* actress plays the following moment. *She stands outside the door with the keys in her hand, she fumbles through the key ring until she finds the one that opens the door, she puts it in the lock, and she fiddles with it the way she knows she must in order to get the habitually stuck door open. As she opens the door she intends to immediately look toward her answering machine to see if her personal trainer, who she kind of has a crush on (even though he's married), has called. But she senses an odd presence across the room. She looks up, sees a roomful of people, and feels herself flush at first with fear until she recognizes a few happy and familiar faces and hears them shout, "Surprise!" She puts down her keys, takes in more faces, tries to relax herself, and finally says, "Holy shit."*

Here's the way the bad actress plays the moment. *She puts the key in the lock, opens the door, looks at the roomful of people, waits for them to shout surprise, and says, "Holy shit."*

The director Mike Nichols said that one of the best lessons he ever had about acting came from something he heard Lee Strasberg say in critiquing a scene. Strasberg asked the actress who had just done a scene (poorly) how she would go about making a fruit salad, step by step. The girl told him how she would wash the fruit, peel it, dice it, then put it in the salad. Strasberg said, "That's right. But you don't get fruit salad unless you do each step and individually cut each piece. You can't take a steamroller and roll over it. You have to do each piece one by one." Nichols said that what this taught him was that in good acting "there's no shortcut." You have to fully absorb one moment before you go to the next—you can't steamroll over all of it.

The talented actor makes the salad, the untalented one steamrolls. *The talented actor hits twenty notes with exactitude in the space of time the untalented actor hits five.*

Practice throughout the day doing the smallest dramatic actions, doing them with a lot of notes, and doing each note completely. Think of these as "etudes" or the five-finger exercises a pianist might do. That way, when it comes time to rehearse a real role, your ability to play a lot of notes will be well honed, and you won't have to overanalyze individual moments, which can make an actor self-conscious.

## Emotion is the end of tension

If actors were able to pick one aspect of acting talent they could always have available to them, most would choose *emotion*. The job of acting is really a piece of cake when the emotions are flowing freely. Consequently actors are always looking for emotion and are often hyperaware of its presence or absence. (Actors are the only people who could be crying their eyes out at a funeral while actually thinking to themselves, "Now why couldn't I do *this* in the O'Neill play I did last month?")

Ironically, sometimes, in an actor's *zeal to feel*, he or she can unknowingly *sabotage* the ability to generate emotion.

When actors want too desperately to feel—if the feeling doesn't come right away—they start to manufacture it *by squeezing and tensing their bodies*. This approach usually only works up a facsimile of emotion that is all physical and is forced, emotion that I call "actor feeling."

Here's how "actor feeling" looks: your face contorts, your muscles tighten, your abdomen stiffens, your knees bend, your voice chokes, and all your emotion comes out in pants and other assorted breathing ticks that Hamlet described as "the windy suspiration of forc'd breath." It may *seem* like feeling to the actor, but it's not real feeling. As Paul Rudnick once said about such acting: "One must never confuse talent with asthma."

When you tense your body to make emotion, what you do is actually the opposite of what happens in real life when you feel. Look at newspaper photos of people who are being emotional (pictures of war zones, disasters, funerals, etc.). Notice what they are doing with their bodies. Even though they may be in extreme emotion, if you look closely, you won't see their bodies tensing. Their bodies will, instead, appear to be "relaxing." They seem to be collapsing, surrendering—as if they are letting go of something.

Real emotion is not tense; *real emotion is the end of tension*.

Notice even the language we use to describe strong emotion. We say things like: *I broke down, I fell apart, I fell in love, I spilled my guts, I was blown away, I caved, I lost it, I had a meltdown, I exploded, I was devastated, I was shattered.* All images of releasing, not of strain. We don't say: *I was so upset I built up!* Or *I climbed in love!* Or *my guts stayed in!*

Emotion doesn't have to be worked up because it's already in your body, trapped there by tension. In essence, *tension is the process by which we try to control emotion with our bodies.* But when you let that tension go, the natural emotion is released. As any masseuse or yoga instructor can tell you, when people loosen up tensed muscles, they frequently have strong, unexplainable emotions rise up.

*The looser the body, the freer the emotion.* Take a look at kids and drunks, for instance. Both have loose, untense bodies (by the way, if ever you need to play a drunk, study the way a three-year-old walks, moves, sits, etc.). They both also have more access to their emotions than adults or sober people do.

A three-year-old can cry at the drop of a hat. But he can also fall down with such force the whole backyard shakes, and then get up and smile. Loose body, free emotions. The same is true of drunks. Alcohol relaxes and loosens the body, which is why we always hear of the drunk being the only one in the car accident to walk away with no broken bones. After a drunk becomes physically free and even starts to get a little "sloppy," he or she often has all kinds of trapped feelings come out. *"I just wanna say how much I love you guys!"*

The equation of *loose bodies* equaling *free emotions* has been known to all the best acting theorists. Stanislavski, the father of so-called Method acting, had his first major brainstorm about how to teach actors the way to access emotion by observing how emotionally free actors used their bodies:

> I felt the presence of something that was common to all of them, something by which they reminded me of each other. It was easiest of all for me to notice this likeness in their physical freedom, in the *lack of all strain*. Their bodies were at the beck and call of their inner demands.

The same was true for Lee Strasberg of Actors Studio fame and the most famous teacher of Method acting in America, a man with an almost infamous reputation for getting actors to use real emotion in their work. Strasberg made actors spend months sitting in a chair, doing monologues with their bodies utterly limp as he walked around lifting limbs and letting them flop back down. All so that actors would stop "holding" tension in their bodies. No one was allowed to get up and perform those famously emotional scenes at the Actors Studio until they had first worked diligently to rid themselves of physical tension.

It was a point Strasberg drove home to actors with such vigilance that one of his famous pupils described a dream he once had in which he was lying dead in his coffin. Lee Strasberg comes over to the coffin, lifts the actor's lifeless arm, lets it drop back down, and says, "Still too tense!"

## Intelligence is part of acting talent

When he was told that an actor he knew took a gun and "blew his *brains* out," Noel Coward responded, "He must have been a good shot."

A stereotype has it that actors aren't the smartest people in the world. Not only are actors *not* considered intellectual, but there is a belief that actors *shouldn't* be intellectuals—that intellect somehow undermines emotion or spontaneity. For years actors have been told by directors and acting teachers things like "Stop thinking!" Or "Get out of your head!"

The stereotyping is based on a complete misunderstanding. What these directors and acting teachers are really saying is: Don't think about *yourself* or *your performance*!" Or, "Get *yourself* out of your head!" What was meant as a warning against self-consciousness has turned into the mistaken belief that intelligence is incompatible with good acting.

But this notion runs counter to what great drama is all about and what great dramatic characters represent. The best dramatic characters are people who have lived for, and in some cases died for, an *idea*, a belief. While these characters may undergo emotional turmoil, what makes them rise to a level of greatness is the *wisdom* of what they are feeling and their conscious understanding of that belief.

When Blanche DuBois defends her "delusions," she tells Mitch:

> I don't want realism! I want magic! Yes, yes, magic!
> I try to give that to people. I misrepresent things

to them. I don't tell the truth, I tell what ought to be truth. And if that's sinful, then let me be damned for it!

She is not just a distraught individual. She is a philosopher of the heart, the personification of an idea, the voice of all those who have ever sacrificed themselves for an illusion.

Since great drama is always about giving the audience a piece of hard-won intellect, you can't give a *great* performance of a role unless you are an actor who can be *passionate about an idea.*

Most actors naturally have what psychologists call *emotional intelligence.* As a result, actors can be just as insightful about a character from literature as any scholar can be—often more so. It's a shame to waste this acumen by being skittish about reading and interpreting literature, but many actors are. They feel they haven't "read enough" and, ironically, allow this insecurity to *prevent* them from reading much. Which, to me, is as absurd as someone refusing to go to a gym because they aren't in shape.

Trust your actor's intelligence and use it in your performances. Don't be afraid to add to it by reading as much as you can; read with your emotional intelligence; read to *feel*; read because it is your job to *embody* great ideas; and, finally, read because—as C. S. Lewis describes the experience of it—reading is a very actorly endeavor, an exercise in becoming.

In reading great literature I become a thousand men and yet remain myself. Like the night sky in the

Greek poem, I see with myriad eye, but it is still I who see. Here as in worship, in love, in moral action, and in knowing, *I transcend myself; and am never more myself than when I do.*

## When you concentrate, it should feel good

I once saw a self-portrait that Marilyn Monroe sketched of herself all hunched over like she had the weight of the world on her. The caption she wrote at the bottom of it was "I must concentrate." A lot of actors feel this way. They think concentration is a chore, the mental version of bench pressing.

And you can *see it* on them.

If I showed you a film of an actor rehearsing a monologue while being coached by an off-camera director—even with the sound off—you would probably be able to tell the moment when the actor started to "act" and the moment when he or she "stopped acting" to take in information from the director. Because when actors start to act, their effort at focusing often registers on their faces. There is a slight but perceptible strain that happens as soon as they begin to "concentrate."

In reality, if you are concentrating *correctly*, the opposite should be true. It should be easy; it should feel pleasurable. If you think about it, most of what we do for recreation are activities that demand great concentration: from sports, to video games, to crossword puzzles, to knitting. But we don't think of concentrating on those activities as being difficult because we find them interesting. And that's the secret!

*In order to concentrate on something when you act, it has to be something that you really want to think about, otherwise your brain won't do it willingly.*

It has to be something that keeps *you* absorbed. So at times you may have to think of something (analogous but) different from what your character might. Rather than trying to concentrate on Juliet's moonlit face that Romeo talks about, you may have to think of something more erotic. Rather than trying to concentrate on the cherry orchard the family is about to lose, you may need to think of the lyrics of a song you love as you look out the window. Do whatever it takes to find an object of concentration that is absorbing and enjoyable.

Second, you need to be sure you have *enough* material to keep you engaged. The brain is like a garbage disposal: it devours quickly and looks for more. If an actor has to look at a cherry orchard for five minutes, his brain will grow bored in about fifteen seconds unless he keeps feeding it interesting morsels.

Again, take a lesson from kids. They actually concentrate *better* than adults. They can stay focused for hours as long as the toys are stimulating enough.

So find stimulating "toys" and concentration will be easy. And if it's not easy, it means you're doing it wrong.

I know an older actor who played the role of a batty old uncle in a play. The character was busy writing his "memoirs" during the play. During rehearsals and into the long run of the play, the actor *actually wrote* the fictitious memoirs of the character! Some nights he became so engrossed in his writing that he almost missed his cues. But his performance was unforgettable and charmingly real. By the end of the run he had amassed hundreds of pages of a quite fascinating memoir. Now that's concentration.

## Talent has nuance

A lot of times, during an audition, a director will ask an actor to make an "adjustment" to his or her performance as a way of testing how well the actor can "take direction." What the director is looking for is an actor who can execute a piece of direction with *nuance* and not go for heavy-handed extremes.

Here's an example. I once worked with actors on the last scene of Chekhov's play *The Seagull,* in which the characters of Constantin and Nina say goodbye. The girl playing Nina hugged the other actor with such forced intensity she almost broke his collarbone. I said, "Try it again, and don't hug him quite so hard." But the next time she did it she went *too far in the other direction*, she hugged him so lightly it looked like she was embracing someone who had a bad sunburn. On an intensity scale of 1 to 10, she went from a 10 to a 1.

Jumping between the extreme of 10 to 1 or from 1 to 10 is what bad actors do. (Maybe, on a good day, from a 9 to a 2.) But good actors go for the more nuanced levels: the 3, 4, 5, and 6s.

One way to get more nuance in your acting is to use something I call *mini-thoughts*. At every waking moment, people's minds are a constant stream of small thoughts—thoughts they aren't even fully conscious of having. You hug the widow at the funeral and try to move your head so that her hair gel doesn't smudge your glasses. You get bad news on the phone and still think to pull off your earring so the phone doesn't make it dig into your ear. These are mini-thoughts.

While they may not seem important, they can add a lot to your acting. They'll give nuance to your behavior, because they cause us to make small shifts in how we do things.

Let me go back to *The Seagull* scene. I finally told the actors that while they hugged each other they should notice something about the other person, some "mini-thought" observation like thinking about the temperature of the other person's body, the scent of the hair, the feel of the body they are pressing against, etc. Something to engage the mind and cause it to respond to the nuance of the moment.

## Love is part of technique

Love is one part of acting talent that is difficult to talk about without sounding sappy. But it's an important part of an actor's technique. In my experience, when a performance is bad it's usually because there was no real love present, either within the actors or between them.

Audiences *love* real love. Anytime an actor seems to have real love for someone or something, an audience will follow him or her forever. It doesn't always have to be love between two people; and it doesn't always have to be a love that's noble or even good. Richard III may love power or cruelty or himself, but when audiences watch an actor really "love to be bad" they are just as happy watching *that* as they are watching any good love story!

In a way all good drama is about *conflicts of love*, so the actor who can't bring real love to the stage will never be able to embody the conflicts of great drama. That's why you need to think of love as an important part of your acting technique.

As soon as you start work on a project and meet the actors you'll be working with, look for some aspect of each actor that you can love in a similar way to how your character loves his or her character. If someone is playing your mother, try to imagine sitting on the actress's lap thirty years ago; if someone is playing your spouse, imagine the way the actor looks when asleep. But never, ever tell the other actors what you are doing because the secrecy of it increases the power of the feelings—as secrecy always does. (And you don't want colleagues thinking you're a stalker.)

But if you try working this way you will be surprised what a strong, secret feeling you can get for someone who weeks before was a total stranger. And most people, no matter who they are, have some trait you can find to love.

Occasionally you may be stuck working with someone whom your character is supposed to love, and whom you simply cannot stand. Time and again I hear actors complain about the person they are playing opposite. Without question it's easier to have feeling for someone you really care for. But don't let yourself off the hook by blaming another actor if a scene isn't working.

Keep a couple of things in mind. First of all, if you are a *good enough* actor you should be able to crack through whatever shell the other actor is putting up, at least a little bit. *A talented actor makes other actors more talented.* I doubt if there is any actor on earth who wouldn't open up more than usual when working with a Meryl Streep or a Robert De Niro. So try to prove your talent to yourself by making the horrible person across from you better. And remember, no audience member ever says, "I thought the actor who played the son was bad, but I can't blame him because he probably wasn't being fueled by the girl who played his sister."

If you are really having a tough time with another actor and can't seem to work up any feelings toward that person, here is a good way to help you create some kind of love for someone you dislike. This may sound odd, but here's what you do—and if you try it you'll see that it works. You picture something very terrible and very painful happening to the person. Imagine the worst thing you can think of: fire, torture, or the worst trauma imaginable; and imagine it happening in *great detail.* What you'll find is that people have a natural empathy for *any* human being who is being badly hurt, regardless of who they are. We have deeper reservoirs of human connection—and yes, love—that can be activated by imagining something along these lines.

An actor friend of mine also told me recently that sometimes he thinks of the other actor as a small child. This too can be a way to play on that human instinct to love the vulnerable.

---

## Summary of Notes on Talent

1. *Talent begins in sensitivity.*
2. *Acting is mixing molecules.*

3. *Try to tap your unconscious.*
4. *Acting is tricking your brain.*
5. *The more talented actor hits more notes.*
6. *Emotion is the end of tension.*
7. *Intelligence is part of acting talent.*
8. *When you concentrate, it should feel good.*
9. *Talent has nuance.*
10. *Love is part of technique.*

---

# CHAPTER THREE

# REHEARSAL

## Don't take the watch apart

> "I think the greatest enemy to good theatre is a table."—Peter Brook

Most actors have been forced to begin a rehearsal process with everyone in the show sitting around a table, discussing the script for days on end. At times this can be useful, but frankly it tends to be more helpful for the director than for actors. It can, at times, actually be bad for actors. They can get to like sitting around that table. It can become a security blanket, a way of avoiding the scary part of the actor's work, which is getting up on your feet and trying to "feel" all the analysis you've been gabbing about.

Worst of all, too much of this kind of thing in a rehearsal process can make actors start "taking the watch apart."

By this I mean that, at the end of this "table work," the play and the character can be broken apart into a lot of isolated bits and pieces and fragmented ideas. This can make an actor confused, frustrated, and sometimes panic-stricken.

While the goal of text analysis should be to *stimulate* an actor into feeling, too much information or "data" about a character can immobilize rather than stimulate you. As the writer Elias Cannetti, put it, "Asking too many questions is death to a person who feels."

Of course you want to ask questions about your character, but I would try to avoid having some pre-set template of questions that you ask about every single text, even if an acting teacher has taught you that it's blasphemy not to do so. It's better to tailor your question to the specific show. *"How did you feel about your father when you were younger?"* is a good question to ask if you're playing Hedda Gabler but not of much use if you're playing one of the Pigeon sisters in the *The Odd Couple*.

Above all, when you do ask questions, do so because you are looking for stimulation and for *feeling,* not in a spirit of too much analysis (a word, I might add, that fittingly begins with "anal"). Don't be anal about character data. The overly analytical approach can short-circuit intuition. I recently read an interview with Oscar winner Frances McDormand in which she said, "I don't prepare. I learn my lines the night before a scene, because I trust my *intuition* about a woman's behavior." And I thought to myself, "Good for her!" All in all, it's probably better to err on the side of underrehearsing rather than overdoing it and taking the watch apart.

If you *do* find the watch coming apart, try to find ways of reminding yourself that characters are human beings, not data. Go looking for a connection to something living, something organic and real.

I knew an actress who was playing Viola in Shakespeare's *Twelfth Night*. In rehearsals she had been working a lot on the famous "willow cabin" speech—a beautiful verse about what it means to be loyal forever to the love of your life. The actress analyzed the text from every possible angle until it became a disjointed hodgepodge that lacked feeling.

One day the director showed her something he found in the morning newspaper. It was a little clipping he had cut from the obituary section. It had been placed by a widower who, the year before, had lost his wife of fifty-two years. It was simply the dates of their marriage, the date of his wife's death, and the entire text of the Willow Cabin speech. The actress was so touched by this that she taped the clipping to the mirror of her dressing room. It put a human face on "the watch," as I call it, and helped her put the bits and pieces of it back together again.

## If you rehearse too fast, you'll perform too slow

Next time you are at a performance of a show you don't think is very good, try this experiment. Close your eyes and listen. Notice how much *pausing* goes on, how much dead air there is between and "within" the lines. I have a friend I often go to the theater with, and time and again, if the show is bad, I just point to my ear and she knows what that means. "Close your eyes and listen to the pauses." We always laugh, because it's uncanny how often excessive pausing is at the core of bad shows.

Occasionally a director will point this out to actors. But often this does not make actors pause less. It just makes the actors push and rush when they are not pausing.

The time and place to lay the groundwork for preventing one of these pause-a-thon performances is, believe it or not, *in rehearsal.*

Actors who pause too much, or for too long, are taking the time to do in performance what they should have taken the time to do in rehearsal. They are essentially *rehearsing* in front of an audience. Each pause is a sort of a "micro-rehearsal" of a moment.

Such pauses are not feeling; they are an actor's *attempt* at feeling.

The reason these actors do what I call "rehearsing in performance" is because they were probably *performing in rehearsal.* This comes from rushing to a desired effect rather than have it grow naturally. When you see actors do a scene in class that isn't very good, and you ask them how they rehearsed, often they will say, "Oh, we ran through it a bunch of times." This means they "performed" the scene several times without really rehearsing it. Rehearsal should be less about you running through the play and more about allowing the play to *run through* you, to absorb it in digestible doses over time.

Actors should try not to put on their "performance hat" too soon in rehearsal. That's why I have always believed rehearsals should be closed to outsiders. When someone who is not in the show comes in to "check out" rehearsals, the actors usually notice. They begin *making* moments rather than using rehearsal to take the time to *find* the moments. They skip over the calibrations of character and skim on feeling in their zeal to look good.

If I were asked to give a working definition of rehearsal, I would say it's when an actor tries to discover and experience the changes that a character undergoes throughout a story. Change is the essence of drama: the bigger the change, the bigger the drama. Lose your house keys: small change, small drama. Lose your *house*: bigger change, bigger drama. A dramatic text is nothing more than a *transcript of change*, and the "arc" (a word I can't stand) of a character is just a fancy way of describing the changes the character undergoes. For an actor, the goal of the rehearsal should be to identify the *points of change* that your character undergoes in the script as a whole and then in the individual scenes and moments.

Amazingly, actors are often so keyed up to show off, they don't pause enough in rehearsals. When an actor I am working with must hear a line that changes his character (e.g., "Big Daddy, you have cancer."), I often tell him to take at least a full thirty seconds before responding with his line. The human brain won't allow emotion to be felt right away, because part of its function as a physical defense mechanism is to deflect bad news. That's why the first word out of the mouth of someone who's been given bad news is often "No!" But actors have trouble doing this in rehearsal. They can be so itchy to "perform," to "show" Big Daddy's reaction, that they pause for barely ten seconds. Even after you point it out and ask them to do it again, they take only maybe twenty seconds.

Slow down in rehearsal. Take the time to feel what your character should feel. When it comes time to perform you'll be glad you did, and so will your audience.

## *Instead of the "objective," look at loves and fears*

Some actors call it the "objective," some call it "the action" or "the action verb." It's always been a staple of American acting that an actor must have a strong motivation behind everything his or her character does. Pick up any American acting student's script and you're likely to find "to oppose," "to overtake," or similar snappy infinitives written in the margin next to almost every line.

While there is some merit to this approach, it can also be a problem. One can become unnecessarily specific, like putting next to the line "Please, pass the salt," *to request.* Or one can be painfully obvious, like an actor playing Hamlet who writes next to "To be or not to be," *to question* (gee, good guess). Or one can be ridiculously cerebral, like—lest you think I'm making this stuff up—an actor I knew who put next to the line "Kiss me . . ." that his objective was *to associate.* (Not much of a kisser, that one.)

One of the biggest drawbacks to this verb-in-the-margin stuff is that it can cause you to be on stage and suddenly find yourself thinking more about what you wrote down in your script than about the real-live actor who's standing right in front of you.

I also find that this objective-obsession (and the "*I must get what I want!*" pitch it can give to a scene) can make for a performance that has a kind of forced, generic intensity to it. The acting version of pushy show-tune singing.

Rather than pay attention exclusively to what your character's objective is, try considering two other issues: what your character *loves* and what your character *fears*.

The fact is, in real life people don't always know what their objective is. We often have no idea what we want. You, for example—what is your objective right now? To read? To get information? You're probably not sure. But I bet you could tell me right off the bat what or who you love. And if you took a minute or two, you could also rattle off a hierarchy of your fears.

People *always* know what they love, in both big or small ways: a person, a pet, a restaurant, a band. And they always know what they fear, in big and small ways: disease, rejection, traffic tickets, mice. These two forces tend to be more "present" for us than the notion of the objective. Ultimately, fear may be the most *common* human motivation of all, and love the one that's most *important* to us. Knowing these two aspects of your character will give your scenes some of the undercurrent, "edginess," and passion that acting teachers who endorse the "find-your-objective" method are looking for.

I also find it adds more humanity to your character.

## Memorize only one or two lines at a time

Many actors memorize their lines only superficially, meaning they assume they "have them down," and in many cases can repeat them word for word. But when they get on stage they still "see" the image of the actual words as they appear on the page of the script in their mind. It's almost like they were still reading the words mentally rather than living them. Superficial memorization causes a tentativeness to creep into the voice that has the ring of bad acting to it. There is a subtle but noticeable quality that poorly memorized lines incite in an actor's voice.

The cause of superficial memorization is attempting to memorize too much of a text in one sitting. Often an actor will work on a speech while driving to rehearsal and be letter-perfect in the car, only to get into rehearsal and forget most of the speech in trying to do it off book. How many times have you heard an actor say in frustration, "Damn, I knew this!"?

Memorization is all about creating *connections*.

If, for example, I tell you that my father's astrological sign is Gemini and that my mother's is Virgo, chances are you're not going to remember that for very long. Unless *you* happen to be either a Gemini or a Virgo. In which case you probably will remember it. Or, if I give you two phone numbers to remember and the first one is 555-*8129* and the second one is 555-*1982*, chances are you'll find the second one easier to remember, because it looks like a date, and maybe you were born in 1982 or the year before, or have some other association to it.

We remember things that *connect back to ourselves*. Human memory is, you might say, a very *self*-absorbed mechanism.

In order to "own" your lines, you have to force yourself to make some kind of personal connection with the specifics of what they say and mean. To do that, don't bite off more lines than your personal memory can chew in one sitting.

*Instead of trying to learn too many lines at once, memorize one or two lines at a time.*

Grab a line before you get into the shower, for example ("Whether 'tis nobler in the mind to suffer the slings and arrows of outrageous fortune . . .") And, while you shower, turn that one line over and over in your head, and keep doing it while you eat breakfast and walk the dog. And as you do it keep finding images that *connect the words to you.* Ask yourself what "slings" and "arrows" you have coming at you in *your* life, and think about which are "slings" and which are "arrows," and even why you might use those words to describe them. Do this sort of mental chewing on just *one line at a time*, and don't go to the next line until you have really "worked" the first one.

If you do this throughout a day, by nightfall you'll have all of "To be or not to be" memorized, and because you connected it to yourself and didn't do it superficially, it will stay memorized. And when it comes time for you to perform it, it will be yours.

A final word about memorization. We tend to remember things that (a) tell a *logical story* and (b) touch us in a *physical* or sensual way.

If, for example, you have to remember three random things in order—e.g., a staple, a paper clip, a rubber band, or wine, beer, water—the way to remember them is by making up a small story. *"I have a stack of papers I want to put together. I try stapling, but there are too many pages even to fit in the stapler. Then I try a big paper clip—still too many pages to hold securely. So,* *my only choice is to wrap the pages in a <u>rubber band</u>.*" Test it out. A few days from now try to remember these three random things that you just read—in the proper order. I'll bet you'll be able to do it.

Similarly we remember things that register in our bodies. *Someone hits me over the head with a <u>wine</u> bottle, I fall onto the ground, which stinks of stale <u>beer</u>, and pass out. I am awakened when the paramedics come and throw <u>water</u> on me to revive me.*

Again, test it a few days from now and I bet you'll remember.

## Simple research is better than the show-offy kind

I once saw a production of a play about urban poverty. In the program note the director wrote about a field trip that she and the cast had taken to a local soup kitchen where they spent a few days talking with the poor. The program note was very moving. Unfortunately the performance of the play was not.

Oddly, I have found this scenario to be a common one. Actors who have done well-meaning research or "field work" on a role are somehow unable to convert the experience into usable onstage stimuli. Something gets blocked. Often these "fancier" sorts of research, like the excursion this cast took to the soup kitchen, can "objectify" the subjects of the research, as if they were put on display in a human zoo. While trips like these can bring about a temporary sentimentality in the people who take them, the person who cries at the soup kitchen often won't be able to cry on stage.

I have found an odd mechanism inside good actors, a kind of shut-off valve that stops emotion from being available to them whenever an unconscious voice tells them they are exploiting something that is *sacred.* This is why good actors know not to use for an emotional trigger anything from their life that is too profound or too fresh. These things have a kind of "holiness" to them, and something in the soul won't allow them to be sold cheap.

There is nothing wrong with research as long as it is not done in a way that is exploitive or *show-offy.* Research material gathered in a spirit of humility has a better chance of getting down into your unconscious. So, if you do research or "field work," maybe you should do it alone. Or, at least, don't tell anyone about it.

Finally, to return to more basics, a lot of times something simple is more useful to you than something fancy. Unfamiliar things are a lot harder for our brains to process than "everyday" kinds of things. Instead of going to a soup kitchen to interview a homeless person, you could try sleeping one night on the hard floor of your apartment. Or try not eating any food for twelve hours. Or go into your alley and look through the garbage for ten minutes. Simple things sometimes work best.

## Work inside-to-out and outside-to-in

While some actors claim only to work one or the other of these ways, most good actors work, at times, from the *outside-to-in* and at other times from the *inside-to-out.*

Working from the outside-to-in means you develop a character by starting with something physical or external: their clothing, or a gesture, or walk, or maybe a vocal idiosyncrasy, and then, let this outer stimulus soak into you and shape your character's inner life.

For example, while preparing for the role of Marianne, the daughter in Molière's seventeenth-century farce *Tartuffe,* the actress Swoosie Kurtz was having trouble playing this wide-eyed innocent girl who was so subservient to the men in her life. The director Stephen Porter gave her a very clever *outside-to-in* trick to try in rehearsal. He told her to imagine that the character was *on wheels,* being whirled around the stage rather than walking on her own two feet. Not only was this the perfect physicalization of the character's plight, it was also a funny visual image that immediately sparked the brilliantly zany Kurtz. Her performance was hilarious, won raves, and got her a Tony nomination—all because of a nice piece of *outside-to-in* rehearsal work.

The outside-to-in approach can take many forms. A lot of times actors find one small movement, or a kind of "hub" of energy in their body that ignites a whole character. Look, for example, at the work of Johnny Depp. Notice the way he uses his mouth. Almost all his characters seem to grow out of the physical variations he finds in the area of his mouth: his lips, teeth, jaw. He seems to start with that particular area of his body and allows the initial spark it gives him to ignite an entire character. Jim Carrey is another actor who is also a bit of a *mouth* actor. And Laurence Olivier said he always "started with the nose." It can be an effective way to get you started.

Working from the *inside-to-out* means that you start with the inner stuff—psychology, feelings, the psyche—

and let those elements shape your character's outer manner and physicality.

One of the best examples I know is Anthony Hopkins's creation of Hannibal Lecter in *Silence of the Lambs*. He began with the idea that only a person who was cold and dead on the *inside* could be desensitized enough to do Lecter's awful deeds. From this inner idea, Hopkins shaped the outer manner and sound of the character, such as Lecter's eerie stillness and formal movements; and the robotic politeness of his voice— which Hopkins said he based on "Hal," the computer from *2001: A Space Odyssey*; and the deathly iciness of his stare (Hopkins hardly ever blinked in the whole movie!). A brilliant outer embodiment of a complex inner idea.

Do not *impose* either of these two ways of working on yourself at the outset of rehearsal. See what develops naturally. Sometimes a "subtle" character who you'd think would warrant an *inside-to-out* approach surprises you by beginning to *move* or *talk* in a way that sparks you. Just as an "over-the-top" role may emerge from your instincts about an inner sadness that you perceive in the character.

Michelangelo said, "I see an angel in a block of marble, and I chisel till it flies away." The creative process is a constant shift in focus between the angel and the chisel. For the actor, one is their "inside" and one is their "outside," and you can always use both to help get your characters to fly.

Finally, if you find yourself stuck in your creation of the character during rehearsal and need to "shake things up" a little, try switching whatever approach you were using to the opposite one (that is, if you're working outside-to-in, trying going inside-to-out). Try an outside-to-in rehearsal on Wednesday, and on Thursday do it in more of an inside-to-out way.

That little reshuffling of your approach can reignite you and make good surprises happen.

## Props help behavior and emotion

Most people's "stuff" means the world to them. *Things* that are precious to us run a close second to loved ones. (Some people would rescue the golf clubs and the Prada purse before they'd save the spouse.) But more than it merely mattering to us, our stuff expresses us: it's an extension of us—our souls distributed into objects.

Actors have an intuitive understanding of this aspect of human behavior. I have never met an actor who didn't love to use props. Most actors couldn't care less about sets beyond the initial oohs and aahs of first seeing one (whereas directors spend 90 percent of their time on the sets and about 10 percent on props), but give an actor an interesting prop and stand back.

Props can be very helpful in making onstage behavior seem more realistic. Because we use most of the props of our daily life in an involuntary way (we don't have to think about how to eat or drive or get dressed), we use them "unconsciously." So when we use props on stage or in a movie, it gives acting a nice sense of unself-conscious behavior. Even the worst actor on earth who really drinks water on stage can't swallow water *falsely*!

Good directors know this, and the great ones like Mike Nichols have helped actors use props in very advantageous ways. Watch Nichols's film *Who's Afraid of Virginia Woolf?*, starring Elizabeth Taylor. Taylor was, in my opinion, always more of a "movie star" than a top-notch actress, but in this movie she gives the best performance of her career and one of the best ever on film.

When you watch Taylor in it, notice how there is almost no time in the film that she isn't using props: smoking, swilling booze, gnawing a chicken leg, fondling her jewelry, hurling clothes around her sloppy house. Nichols kept her continually busy with props. Because Taylor's concentration was shifted onto those props, it was taken off herself and, as a result, her usual actressy coyness was stopped. She gave her least self-aware and most character-driven performance ever— and won an Oscar for it.

Above all, props can be a highly effective way for an actor to deepen emotion. Again, something tragic is too large an idea for the brain to take in; whereas simple, everyday objects can be small enough to get past the brain and trip the controls of emotion.

I read a newspaper article about a cop whose partner was shot and killed in the line of duty. He maintained his composure as the paramedics came and worked on his partner. It wasn't until he saw in his partner's shirt pocket a Garfield the Cat pen (that had been given to the slain cop by his kid) that the full emotion finally blindsided him. A shooting, a dead friend, and a fatherless kid were too much for his brain to take in— but the Garfield pen got through.

## *It's all right to use a crutch*

Smoking a cigarette, eating, playing with a prop, wearing a costume piece, experimenting with some physical tic—these are all acting crutches, things actors do when they're stuck while rehearsing a role and need a little help.

"Crutch" is a word with a negative connotation. People say things like, "You are just using such and such as a *crutch!*" My feeling is: so what! What's wrong with a crutch if it can help you? Using a crutch is a perfectly legitimate rehearsal technique.

I once saw an actor rehearse the fast-moving farce *Noises Off,* and every time he was out of sight of the "audience" he hopped around on one leg in order to give himself more of a sense of being overwhelmed by the chaotic circumstances of the play. The actor was trying to get that same sense of panic and peril on stage in the show. He ended up being both believable and hilarious in the role. Good crutch.

I saw an actress do the 1930s comedy *The Front Page.* In rehearsal she chewed wads of bubble gum to give her more of a sense of the clipped and snappy way of speaking in a play that took place in 1930s Chicago. She didn't ultimately do it in the show, but a few days of rehearsing with gum helped her tune into the style of the play. Good crutch.

Sometimes if a crutch is a good one, it will end up being used in the show. Everyone knows about the cotton balls Marlon Brando stuffed in his cheeks for *The Godfather.* But during rehearsal he also wore earplugs in order to help him feel the character's age and growing alienation from the world around him. And he ended up using them in his scenes in the movie.

Be creative. But also be professional and don't do something tacky. The actor who shows up to a rehearsal for *Macbeth* wearing a kilt has missed the point. Bad crutch.

The best rehearsal crutches of all are ones that no one can see you using.

## Don't overrehearse the big moments

Most good roles have at least one "big moment" in them. Like the character of Linda in *Death of a Salesman* who has the famous "attention must be paid" speech, in which she angrily defends her husband against the disrespect of her sons.

Because these moments are so important to the play or the movie, and often to the actor as well, actors are inclined to think about them and worry about them too much and, worst of all, *rehearse* them too much.

The first few times you do the big scene or big speech in rehearsal, everyone is blown away, partly because they are hearing it for the first time. But over the course of rehearsal you end up doing it so many times that it naturally starts to lose its sizzle. Then the actor starts thinking that the scene has "lost" something. And, for an actor, there is no hell on earth like thinking your performance has lost something it once had.

You will have to rehearse the big moment enough in the regular course of the rehearsal process, so don't rehearse it on your own—ever. You'll drain the life out of it. Also be assured that a good director will understand

this and won't force you to keep doing the scene too often. If you have a director who keeps pressing you to do
it again and again, simply ask if you can try to conserve
a little for performance. That way the director will
know that you are deliberately holding back, rather
than assuming you are not able to "get there" anymore.
Boxers have an expression for it. They say, "Don't leave
it in the gym."

*In your own mind, pay very little attention to the big
moment and more attention to the little moments that
lead up to it.*

"Big moments"—both on stage and in life—are really
just the point at which a lot of *little moments* that have
been building up burst forth. The big moment in a play
should feel like taking your hands off the handlebars of
your bicycle as you soar downhill: if you are *up to speed*
it's the easiest thing in the world to do. And it's all the
small moments that get an actor up to speed. If Linda
Loman has spent the first hour of the show noticing all
the small ways in which her boys show disrespect for
their father—a thousand tiny glances between the actors throughout—it won't be hard for her to erupt at her
sons and demand that "attention must be paid."

## Never neglect the practicals

Every director you work with will have a different way
of rehearsing. Some will give hyperspecific directions;
some will all but leave you totally alone. Some will discuss character motivations endlessly; others will say little about "character" and will concentrate instead on
stage pictures. Some directors will be as organized as
engineers; others will thrive on chaos. It's your obliga-

tion as a professional to be flexible and cooperative, because nothing stamps an actor as "difficult" more quickly than having too rigid an idea of what *you* think rehearsal should or shouldn't be, and nothing damages a rehearsal atmosphere like an actor who is openly adversarial to a director.

That said, there is one aspect of the preparation for a performance that you must always make sure the director gives you. It's what I call "the practicals."

These are anything in the preparation of a role that require *organization and precision* (such as line memorization), or working out *intricacies of coordination* (like prop or costume organization, both on stage and backstage), or the acquisition of any skill that requires technical drill (like accents or fight choreography).

Don't allow the director to neglect these practical things in rehearsal. Eventually it will be your ass out there. You'll be stuck on the *Titanic,* and the director will be like the guy who dressed in drag and hopped on a lifeboat. So get what you need to have the practicals go smoothly.

Directors aside, don't *you* get so artsy-fartsy, touchy-feely in rehearsal that you end up being the one to neglect them. When practical things go wrong in a performance, they can do a lot more damage than simple bad acting. There are no anecdote books written about actors who didn't act as well as they could have, but there have been several amusing collections of stories about theatrical screwups. So remember: five acts of feeling Romeo's pain will all come crumbling down if, in the Act V graveyard scene, you forget to bring on your sword and have to kill Paris by giving him a karate chop.

## Summary of Notes on Rehearsal

1. *Don't take the watch apart.*
2. *If you rehearse too fast, you'll perform too slow.*
3. *Instead of the "objective," look at loves and fears.*
4. *Memorize only one or two lines at a time.*
5. *Simple research is better than the show-offy kind.*
6. *Work inside-to-out and outside-to-in.*
7. *Props help behavior and emotion.*
8. *It's all right to use a crutch.*
9. *Don't overrehearse the big moments.*
10. *Never neglect the practicals.*

# PERFORMANCE

## *Think of the word "act" as being short for actual*

Thinking of the word "act" as being short for "actual" is a good notion to keep in mind as you get ready to perform a role, on stage or in film. When good actors act, they seem to be *actually* doing whatever it is the character does. As Humphrey Bogart once said about Spencer Tracy: "Spencer does it, that's all. Feels it, says it. Talks. Listens. He means what he says when he says it, and if you think that's easy, try it!"

It's not easy. In fact it's very hard to just do things "actually." That's why actors often look more like they are *trying* to do something than actually doing it.

Notice how bad acting has a definite body language to it that comes from not doing things in a way that is actual. I could make two twenty-second silent films—one of a bad actor and one of a good actor—consisting of nothing more than the actors walking onto a stage, taking a newspaper from a table, sitting in a chair, and beginning to read. From that small, silent piece of footage, it would be obvious to everyone who saw it which actor was good and which was bad. The bad actor would walk with a quality that one might describe as "walkness." And he'd sit with a kind of "sitness," meaning the bad actor does everything in a kind of physical *italics*.

Audiences can spot this sort of thing, at least on a subliminal level. They won't say, "Hey, that actor's sitting with sit-ness!"—it will just look like the actor is tentative, lacking command.

As an old director I knew used to say, "Look like you *belong*." But to do this actors literally have to retrain themselves to do things publicly the way they do them privately. In *An Actor Prepares,* Stanislavski wrote:

> Remember this: all of our acts, even the simplest, which are so familiar to us in everyday life, become strained when we appear behind the footlights before a public of a thousand people. That is why it is necessary to correct ourselves and learn again to walk, move about, sit, or lie down. It is essential to reeducate ourselves to look and see and to listen and hear.

On stage you want to shake yourself out of the zombified "nonawareness" of one's physical reality that makes actors move tentatively and come across falsely.

In *real life* human beings are automatically aware of the *actuality* of their physical relationship to their environment and the objects in that environment. That's because we are always, intuitively, in search of increasing our physical comfort. One need only watch the elaborate rituals people go through on airplanes to make themselves at home: pillow stacking, position shifting, blanket yanking, armrest hogging, etc. In everyday life, minute by minute, we try to make ourselves more physically comfortable by making all kinds of habitual shifts of weight and position.

People do this no matter what the situation is. In the 1920s a Chicago crime reporter told a story about a criminal who was being walked up the steps of the gallows to be hanged. He paused on one wooden step that wobbled under his foot, turned to the executioner, and said, "Is this thing safe?"

Even to the last, human beings interact in an actual way with their environment. Even sitting in the electric chair, a person would shift his weight if some part of the chair were digging into him uncomfortably. When actors get on stage, however, they sometimes shut off this natural mechanism and view a constant, low-grade, physical discomfort as the norm.

Work at getting this sense of physical actuality to what you do on a stage or a set. Before a show, go out and spend some time on the set. Sit around and do basic human tasks out there on the stage. Sit, read, eat takeout on the set for *Romeo and Juliet*—they ate back then, you know! Walk around. Feel like you belong. Keep reinforcing for yourself that the set isn't a place "where a show goes on" but someplace where real behavior happens.

Just make sure that, if you do this sort of thing, you don't make a big deal of it or inconvenience people when you do it. (Liza Minnelli supposedly liked to do a little pre-show preparation for her Radio City Music Hall concert in which she would lie down for a while on every single inch of the gargantuan stage to get comfortable with the space. A bit much, I think. All in all, a good rule of thumb is that your pre-show preparation shouldn't scare the stagehands.)

## *Anchor the imaginative to something real*

Performance is the time when you take the imaginative things you've developed in rehearsal and make them concrete for yourself and your audience. In performance you should make every effort to anchor the things you imagined in rehearsal to something or someone physically on stage with you.

Take a look at the most skilled pretenders of all—kids. Notice how, when they play, they always *connect the imaginative to something real*, something they can see, feel, and use. If no toy pistol is handy, they form *their fingers* into the shape of a gun. Or they make the actual *seam in the carpet* be the river of alligators that the plastic army guys cannot cross. They don't just *imagine* the gun and the river, they anchor it to the *real* finger and *real* carpet seam. They make believe by making *belief*. And one never outgrows the instinct to believe what can be seen and touched more than what is merely imagined.

I know an actress who was in a production of *The Diary of Anne Frank*. She spent the rehearsal period "imagining" the Nazi soldiers who eventually find the characters in the play hiding in the attic. In the climactic final scene, the actress was instructed by the director to stand up against a wall stage right in fright. This wall was in a place in the theater where the actress could faintly feel the theater's air-conditioning system rumbling below the stage. She said she'd lean into the wall and listen for that sound and pretend it was the sound of the truck waiting for them downstairs, the truck the Nazis would put her "family" into and take them to concentration camps. She anchored the actual to the real in a way that was very moving for her.

## *You only need enough belief to feel*

Actors often worry about how much belief they need to have in the imaginary circumstances of the play. They sometimes feel a kind of artistic guilt about it and wonder, "Am I *believing* enough, or am I just a faker?"

It's a fair question. Exactly how much belief should you have? When you look out the stage-left window to say the line about the "cherry orchard" that your character is supposedly seeing, should you really *see* a cherry orchard appear like a mirage? Or do you just see what's really there—the potbellied stagehand who's prepping for the next cue? And if you see more "stagehand" than "orchard," does that mean you are not a good actor?

The answer is very simple: *You only need enough belief to make you feel.* Don't worry about how vividly you imagine something, because it doesn't matter as long as it's enough to generate emotion for yourself. That's all. Any actor who tells you he or she completely believes in the circumstances is either a liar or nuts. I have never heard of an actor playing Romeo who was so convinced he was dead at the end of the show that he forgot to get up and take his curtain call.

Simply put, the relationship between *belief* and *feeling* works pretty much the same for the actor as it does for an audience. When an audience watches a movie, they need only enough belief in the circumstances to make them *feel*. No one watching *Titanic* yells, "Oh my God, Leonardo DiCaprio is floating on a piece of ice in the North Atlantic! Quick, somebody call his agent and tell them to have the Coast Guard dispatched!" They know perfectly well that Leonardo DiCaprio is an actor. They know whom he dates, how many millions he's getting for the movie they're watching, and they have even seen pictures in *People* magazine of him filming the very scene they are crying about. But none of this gets in the way of audiences having "just enough" belief to allow them to cry at the plight of the character he plays.

A good phrase that sums all this up was written in 1817 by Samuel Taylor Coleridge. He referred to it as the "willing suspension of disbelief," and it is the ability that gives you (what he called) "poetic faith." Which, to me, means having just enough faith for the poetic feeling of something to touch you.

But this willing suspension of disbelief should be looked on as a tool, not as a test of the authenticity of your acting talent.

## Play to actors, not to their characters

This is the actress Eva Marie Saint on Marlon Brando:

> When you work with other actors, something happens to them when they assume the character. The

eyes grow gray and glassy, the way a snake does before it's going to shed its skin. Actors start acting. Marlon never did.

When great actors act, they don't think of the other actors they act with as though they were characters. They relate to *them*, as people—real people standing right in front of them. Actors like Brando who do this don't get that "gray" look in the eyes that Saint described, because this "glassiness" comes from actors not fully looking at the other actor but instead looking through a kind of imaginary veil of character. And as Saint says, you can *see* this in the look that comes into the actors' eyes when they do it.

When you act with someone, always think: *Do it to the actor, not to the character*. If the character you play is supposed to hurt the other character with the words you say, hurt *the actor* with your words. Try to get the other actor to come backstage and say, "You scared me!" Or if your character wants to seduce the other character, seduce *the actor* on stage—literally. Try to get that actor to come backstage and say, "You know, I'm seeing someone at the moment."

This idea could be thought of as a rewrite of that old term "the actor's instrument." It usually refers to the actor's "self"—body, voice, psyche. But the real "actor's instrument" is *the other actor*. So play them. Play *them*.

## Use changes in status

Bad acting has a *sameness* to it. It doesn't change or grow but stays in one tone and at one level. Next time you encounter bad acting, notice its sameness.

Good acting, on the other hand, has variety. There are changes in color, shifts in tone, and surprises. When you are acting well, this variety comes naturally, but even on those nights when you are feeling less than inspired you can still generate this variety by using a technique developed by the British acting teacher Keith Johnstone.

It's called *status,* and Johnstone's premise is that when people in real life interact with one another there are numerous shifts in what he calls "status." At times Person A *has the status,* and then at times it shifts to Person B and then back again, and so on. An example:

Person A: "How are you?"
Person B: "None of your business."
Person A: "Geez. Sorry . . . Bastard."

The status shifts were: (1) Person A *has the status* because he initiates the interaction; (2) Person B *takes the status* by being adversarial and nasty; (3) Person A *feels his lessened status* when he says, "Geez. Sorry," but then he takes the status back with "Bastard."

Status is about the subtle shifts in power that go on between people. Some are just small, barely noticed shifts:

Person 1: I'm beat. I've been working since seven!
Person 2: *I've* been working since six!

And there are more dramatic shifts, like Hamlet's famous first line that cuts the fawning Claudius down to size.

Claudius: But now, my cousin Hamlet, and my son—
Hamlet: A little more than kin and less than kind.

In the space of two lines, Hamlet goes from humiliated to strong, and Claudius goes from cocksure to deflated.

Playing these subtle or overt power shifts causes little rises and falls in your conversational *energy* that create variety and alleviate sameness. And Johnstone found that actors immediately took to this notion of status.

> "Try to get your status a little above or below your partner's," I said. And the actors seemed to know exactly what I meant, and the work was transformed. The scenes became "authentic," and actors seemed marvelously observant. Suddenly we understood that every inflection and movement implies a status, and that no action is due to chance or "motiveless." It was alarming. All our secret maneuverings were exposed.

I think actors like this little technique because you can up the intensity of their performance quickly, just by using one simple device. You don't have to shred a script into a complex scheme of beat changes and motivations. All you have to do is be aware of the force of *status* that goes on between you and the other actor and you'll naturally add small changes of dynamics, emotional variation, color, and jolts of energy to a performance.

Status may even be used when you are on stage alone, doing a monologue. In fact it should *especially* be used for monologues, because the single biggest trap of a monologue is for an actor to paint the whole thing with a monochromatic wash of sameness.

Some monologues may be a "status fight" between the opposing ideas within the speaker's head. It's "To be" versus "Not to be." And a hell of a good fight it is. At the very least a monologue is almost always a status fight between your character's need to speak his or her mind, and the reluctance to put the feelings into words and speak them out loud.

## *While performing, focus on "the thing itself"*

The plot of Joe Orton's dark comedy *Loot* revolves around characters who are hiding the corpse of an old lady. The first production of the play had been running in London's West End for months when the playwright's mother died. Orton returned home to attend her funeral. When he returned, he visited backstage and told one of the leads they were going to change a prop. In the play, while hiding the corpse, the characters go through all kinds of high jinks with the dead old lady's false teeth. Orton told the actor that instead of the prop teeth they had been using, they would begin using a new set, which he casually placed in the actor's hand. He then announced that they were his dead mother's own teeth which he had gotten from the undertaker!

The actor, realizing he held in his hand the real false teeth of a freshly dead old lady, in Orton's words "turned to jelly." At which Orton scolded him:" It's obvious that you're not thinking of the events of the play in terms of reality, if a thing affects you like this."

Orton taught the actor a good lesson. Often the key to a scene is simply what's right in front of the actor: the situation, the people, the objects, etc. It's what I call "the thing itself." But actors can get so focused on getting an audience to feel what they and the director think they should be feeling in the scene that the actor can go on playing a scene about holding a dead lady's false teeth in his hands for months on end and never let that "thing" fully sink in.

Actors neglect "the thing itself" when they get too wrapped up in the interpretation of a play or scenes. "Interpretation," a production's overall "take" or angle, should probably be uppermost in the mind of the director, but not in the actor's mind—at least not on a conscious level. The writer Susan Sontag claimed that "Interpretation is the intellect's revenge on art," and I think she has a point. *Interpreting is not experiencing; very often it's the opposite of it.* The interpreter observes more than participates, and this is not an optimum vantage point for an actor to get locked into.

When you are performing, keep "interpretation" out of your mind and focus on *the thing itself.* This is always the basic "thing" that the scene is about, be it a person, an object, or a character's issue. More often than not, all the power of a moment is contained in exactly *what it is,* with no need for interpretation.

I once had a talk with an actor who was doing the graveyard scene in a production of *Hamlet.* The director had told everyone that he thought of Yorick's skull as a metaphor for Denmark. But I told the actor, "Forget about Denmark, and just imagine the following. Tonight you go into a graveyard where someone has just dug up the grave of a person you knew and loved, who died twenty years ago. They toss you the decomposed head of your friend, and you look at it. That's it. Play *that* thing."

I mean, after all, is there any interpretation that will be as strong as just that *thing itself*?

(Of course, when the scene improved the next time the actor did it, no doubt the director thought to himself, "Finally, my skull-as-metaphor interpretation is starting to bear fruit!" But what directors don't know won't hurt them.)

## Actors love moments, but audiences love momentum

A good rule of thumb for actors to keep in mind is that rehearsal is the time for the *character*, but performance is the time for the *play*.

It's okay for you to indulge your character in rehearsal. That's the time for it. That's when you should be deeply exploring your character's moments, both in the play and in the character's life beyond the story (as you imagine it). But when it comes time to give the *actual* performance, you have to serve the overall show.

*Don't let your love of a particular "moment" in your performance wreck the momentum of the performance as a whole.* Every role should contribute to the rollercoaster ride of energy that an audience experiences at a performance, and any actor who makes that ride come to an inappropriate halt will be disliked by the audience.

A friend of mine played the lead in a production of Shakespeare's *Henry IV, Parts 1 and 2*. The actor who played his father was an older British actor who was three-parts good actor, one-part huge ham. He was always telling the cast stories of his experiences with "Larry" (Sir Laurence Olivier) and "Dear Orson" (Welles).

In the play there's a famous scene in which the young Prince (played by my friend) gives a moving speech to his dying father, the careworn King—who's lying on a bed. In performance this older actor decided to show what realistic death spasms he could muster up. So while my friend tried his best to do justice to a beautiful monologue, the old ham was busy turning *Henry IV, Parts 1 and 2* into *Look at My Moment, Parts 1, 2, 3, 4, and 5*.

The scene is meant to be a son's touching tribute to the way his father gave his life to his duty: "The care on thee depending hath fed upon the body of my father." All any actor playing the father has to do is lie still and the scene will be a tearjerker. But, in this case, the "body" of the King was so "busy" that the sadness the audience would have felt for a serenely dying King was thrown out the window. All of this, ironically, undermined the audience's genuine feeling toward his character.

The actor had his moment, but *the play* didn't.

## *Beware of your gutter-ball*

A *gutter-ball* (my phrase for it) is a mannerism, or tic, or "tone" that an actor habitually falls back on. Just like a gutter-ball in bowling, it tends to happen when your approach has more *force* than focus. And just like a gutter-ball in bowling, you can fall into this *groove* during a performance—and not get back out of it.

Some gutter-balls are *physical*. Common ones include: making various chopping movements with your arms in sync with your words, pointing your finger, gnarling your hands into claws (women seem to do this more than men), rubbing the palms of your hands together as if you were rolling imaginary dough balls (men seem to do this more than women), pursing your lips, crossing your arms, and doing any number of other things to one's hair, such as grabbing, flipping, and the running-through of fingers.

The most common "physical" gutter-ball of all is what I call *head jutting.* This is when an impassioned actor will push the top half of his or her body forward, away from the bottom half, led by a jutting chin that makes the neck collapse. It's an all-too-common body movement that strips an actor of command. When people really feel passionately about something, they don't jut their head forward, they maintain their position: head and body are both literally and figuratively together when someone means what they say.

Sometimes an actor's gutter-ball can be a certain *emotional tone* that the actor defaults to even though the scene may not call for it. Some common tonal gutter-balls are: hypermanliness (men), perkiness (women), cuteness (men and women), crying (men, women, and children), and a whole host of generic feelings like brooding, vulnerability, hysteria, and sentimentality.

The most common "tonal" gutter-ball of all is simple bitchiness—and men are just as guilty of it as women. It's that unattractive quality of being generically angry about something and coloring everything with a whiny huffiness. It's anger without any real depth of pain, and makes a character come across as miffed or merely frustrated. It's very unsatisfying to watch.

Finally, there is the old-standby gutter-ball of screeching too loud when you are emotional. N*ever go to the limit of your vocal power,* always seem to have "more" in reserve.

Not all mannerisms are gutter-balls. Some mannerisms express your personality, but some are physical tics that merely express your *insecurity*. These kinds of mannerisms *trap* feelings rather than express them, and that's why they're gutter-balls.

Try to find your gutter-ball—ask people if they've noticed anything—and try to control it. It's worth the effort, because audiences won't care about you if you're annoying. Simple as that.

## Find freedom within form

Like the word implies, a per-*form*-ance is a *form*. While you may come out of the rehearsal process with certain things set, every performance, each night of a play, each take of a film scene, is a unique and spontaneous happening. The challenge you have in performance is to maintain the agreed-upon *form* while finding enough freedom within it to keep it spontaneous and fresh. If a performance has *form* without *freedom* it can become dull, but if it has *freedom* without *form* it can be erratic and unsettling to the other actors.

Be clear which things have been *agreed upon* by you and the director and the other actors. The written lines of the text are, more than likely, set. So is much of the movement and many aspects of character psychology. But, all in all, far less is formed than most actors realize. In fact, more actors cling to the *form* than push the envelope of *freedom*.

This doesn't mean you should go overboard and one night suddenly play Juliet as if she doesn't love Romeo but instead has the hots for the Nurse. But don't feel that you have to touch Romeo's hand on the same word of the same speech night after night.

Take musicians as an example. A cellist isn't all of a sudden going to play a Brahms concerto in a salsa rhythm. Nor will he decide to hold his bow in a goofy new way, just to "keep things fresh." But within the established piece of music he will allow his personal connection to the music and what he feels to color what he does to make each night's performance unique.

I once saw a performance of Shaw's *Pygmalion* starring Peter O'Toole. A wonderful old character actress was playing his maid. When she made her entrance she caught her toe on the carpet as she came into the room and ever so slightly tripped before starting her series of lines with O'Toole. Throughout the whole exchange they both maintained their characters, but she had a look in her eyes that said, "He saw me trip," and he had a look in his eyes that said, "She *saw* me *see* her trip!" Between the two of them there was a wonderful, spontaneous glint. They stayed in character and stayed in the scene but made room for the extra little feelings they had about the carpet glitch. They kept the form, but it was free and fun, and I'll never forget it.

## Your life is your warm-up

Group warm-ups are those pre-show exercises in which the cast gets together before a performance, usually forms a circle, and does vocal and physical exercises to "energize for a show."

I have never in my life met a great actor who really liked doing them.

A few points. First of all, I believe no one should be forced to form a circle with other people once they get out of kindergarten. Second, much of what actors are asked to do in warm-ups—like making strange vocal noises, or playing some kind of hippity-hopping game, or (worse) doing an "energy-centering" exercise—is frankly undignified. Making a roomful of professional adults look like a support group for people with crack-induced brain damage is not something that empowers actors. It is something that makes actors feel silly and undermines their power.

Third, there is a kind of New Age sentimentality at the heart of these warm-ups that speaks a lot to "creating a sense of ensemble." That's fine, but while plays may be performed by ensembles, they are made up of individuals: complex, difficult, unique individuals. Good actors tend to be strong individuals, and some strong individuals may not like this sort of enforced group nuzzling.

I confess I have always found it odd to think of an actor who is about to play Richard III linking arms with the cast in a circle and singing "Kumbaya"—twenty minutes before going out on stage and hacking them to pieces. Furthermore, no great dramatic *character* would stand for these warm-ups. Just try asking Willy Loman or Blanche DuBois or Mother Courage to hold hands and go "mah-may-meh-mo-moo."

The biggest drawback to these kinds of warm-ups is that they can make you start "watching yourself" before you even hit the stage. And that's bad. I'm more in favor of the danger and excitement of going out on stage totally cold and waiting for the jolt you get from being hit by the stage lights and the gaze of a big audience. That jolt can send you into the "zone" you're looking for. Like popping the clutch of a car to get it started: BAM! And the engine starts. Try it sometime.

Finally, the truth is, no pre-show exercises will make you a deeper person than you are when you walk through that stage door an hour before the show. If you read the newspaper that day, or tried to feel what someone else felt, or noticed something you had never seen before; or if you daydreamed, or told a lie, or forced yourself to be totally honest about something; if at any time that day you let yourself feel awkward or curious or inspired—then you'll be ready to act. Your warm-up is your life.

## Teach yourself to care and not to care

One night Laurence Olivier gave a performance in the role of Othello that was different and better than any performance of his career. According to his biographer John Contrell:

> His fellow actors were stunned by it, recognizing true genius at work. They were accustomed to being thrilled by his playing, but this was something else. As he made his way to the dressing room, with the audience still cheering, they formed two lines on either side of the passage and applauded him all the way. He swept past in silence and slammed the door behind him. Someone knocked and asked, "What's the matter, Larry? It was great!" He growled back

loudly: "I know it was great, damn it, but I don't know how I did it. So how can I be sure I can do it again?!"

Any actor would have been happy to give such a great performance, even once. But Olivier was upset about it. No doubt because an actor of his caliber knew the awful truth about a great performance, which is that you often have no idea where the hell it came from.

Acting books omit this fact. They make it all sound very simple. As if to say, "Just do A and B and C and a great performance will inevitably result." This can make actors feel like there is something wrong with them when it doesn't happen, as if they were the only persons in the world who had an on-again, off-again relationship with brilliance.

In reality, the gods of acting are much more fickle than books let on. Some days they will reward with a great performance an actor who spent all day nursing a hangover and loathing his or her profession. Other days they will desert an actor who spent all day reading *Respect for Acting* and volunteering at the "Home for Wayward Thespians," and leave that actor hanging when the curtain goes up.

Deep down, actors know this. I think it's the reason they say *Break a leg!* to each other. There are any number of explanations of the origins of this famous phrase. My favorite is that it comes from the Yiddish expression "You should break your leg and neck," which was said to ward off bad luck. Actors say it to convince themselves they don't care if the performance is good. Of course they care if the performance is good. The problem is, if they care too much about it being good, it probably won't be. Good actors pay heed to this.

A line in a T. S. Eliot poem captures what I am getting at. He says, "Teach me to care and not to care." It's a paradox, for sure, and a superstition, perhaps. But for actors this is a technique. And one that often works.

In the end, there is no getting around the fact that every performance will always be a mystery, so actors might as well embrace this reality. The mystery of why some nights are more magical than others will keep you humble on the nights you're marvelous, because you'll know that tomorrow night you could stink. It will also keep you hopeful on the nights you're "off," knowing that tomorrow the magic may be back. The one thing I know for sure about this mysterious force: it seems to elude actors who resent its mysteriousness.

## When you aren't inspired, fall back on clarity

When you are in the midst of one of those performances that you sense is lacking inspiration, the best thing to do is let *the material* do the work for you. "Trust the material" is a note that directors give actors all the time; and actors hate it because they know it can be director code for "stop acting so much." But the truth is, when you don't have "the magic," the material can usually pull you through it.

When those "off-days" come, and they inevitably will, *don't ever worry while you are performing.* Worry at rehearsal, or in the dressing room, or even waiting in the wings to go on. But once you hit that stage and begin to perform, *never worry.* Because then you'll start "pushing," and that will only make things worse. Worrying not only doesn't ever help a performance, it makes it worse. Acting talent thrives best in a worry-free environment and freezes up from worry.

In these situations, *fall back on clarity.*

Just do the material as written. Clarify what your character does and says, and make the important points of the story clear to the audience. When you cannot give a great performance, falling back on clarity will allow you at least to give a *good* performance. Sometimes a solid, clear telling of the story can be plenty for an audience. (When you think about it, people can have a strong emotional reaction to a play just by reading it in book form.)

Furthermore, clarity can be very refreshing in itself, whether uninspired or inspired. This may sound odd, but I have always liked the way plays come across when actors do "line-throughs" of a show: sitting around sprawled on a floor of the green room, running lines. Since the purpose of the line-through is simply to get the words right, and since everyone just wants to get the damn thing over with, the actors don't "act" too much, allowing the script to flow and become refreshingly simple and clear.

---

## Summary of Notes on Performance

1. *Think of the word "act" as being short for actual.*
2. *Anchor the imaginative to something real.*
3. *You only need enough belief to feel.*
4. *Play to actors, not to their characters.*

5. *Use changes in status.*
6. *While performing, focus on "the thing itself."*
7. *Actors love moments, but audiences love momentum.*
8. *Beware of your gutter-ball.*
9. *Find freedom within form.*
10. *Your life is your warm-up.*
11. *Teach yourself to care and not to care.*
12. *When you aren't inspired, fall back on clarity.*

# CHAPTER FIVE

# GREATNESS

*To be great, you can't always need to be good*

In her book *Respect for Acting*, Uta Hagen described the
process of moving from being a *good* actor into being a
*great* actor. For her this transition came as a result of
working with two influential directors, Harold Clurman
and Herbert Berghoff (whom Hagen later married and
with whom she would open HB Studios, one of the most
respected acting schools in New York). By the time Hagen met these two directors she had already achieved
the status of *good* actress; she was known and respected on Broadway.

But, Hagen wrote, she had begun to feel that "something" was missing in her work, something "greater." I
include the whole passage because it's one of my favorite pieces of writing in any acting book:

> Inevitably, in the learning and turning process from
> amateur to professional, I lost some of the love and
> found myself adopting the methods and attitudes of

the "pro." I learned what I now call "tricks" and was even proud of myself. I soon learned that if I made my last exit as Nina in *The Seagull* with full attention on the whys and wherefores of my leave-taking, with no attention to the effect on the audience, there were tears and a hush in the auditorium. If, however, I threw back my head bravely just as I got to the door, I received a round of applause. I settled for the trick that brought the applause. I had thought of myself as a genuine professional who had nothing more to learn, just other parts to make effective. I began to dislike acting. Going to work at the theatre became a chore and a routine way of collecting my money and my reviews. I had lost the love of make-believe. I had lost faith in the character and the world the character lived in.

Hagen started working with Clurman who, according to her, "Took away my tricks." This put Hagen at an interesting crossroads, a crossroads that many good actors find themselves reaching in their development. Hagen could have continued down the safe but superficial path she had been on, or she could take a different approach. This new approach meant she would have to bring "herself" to roles in a way that was more radical and more revealing than ever before. While the end result might be greater acting, to get there Hagen would willingly have to lose some of her tried-and-true tricks, which meant she'd face a period of being scared and unsure of herself and, potentially, "bad."

The good actor who wants to learn to be a great actor must lose, for a time, the quick and easy approval of audiences and fellow actors. George Bernard Shaw once wrote that when you *learn* something, "it feels, at first, as though you *lost* something." Learning *is* losing, losing the known, maybe even losing something good; but on the other side of losing may be greatness.

To be a great actor you must be willing to relinquish the short-term ego gratification of impressing and let the material make a deeper impression on *you*. Greatness begins when you start trying to measure up to your own high standards rather than being satisfied with meeting the standards of admirers.

To finish with Hagen's story, she claimed that she "floundered for a few years" but that eventually her "love of acting was slowly reawakened," at which point she reemerged not only as a *great* actress but as a great teacher of actors.

## Less isn't always more

In the old days the bad theater actor was the show-off, "the ham," the overdoer. While this particular species of bad theater actor is still around, it's his tamer cousin that is now more common. I am referring to what I call the less-is-more actor.

In his advice-to-the-players speech in *Hamlet*, Shakespeare refers to this type of actor. After telling actors not to overdo and "saw the air too much," he immediately follows up with a warning against becoming a less-is-more actor when he says, "Be not *too tame* neither." Less-is-more actors are tame, afraid to come across like they are trying to act. Instead they come across like they are *trying not to act*.

The Hollywood mogul Sam Goldwyn once said, "The secret to acting is honesty; if you can fake that, you've got it made." Less-is-more actors tend to give those kinds of *fake-honest* performances. They have learned over the years to hide behind an easy "naturalness" that is as much of a mask as any other kind, just more subtle.

Many actors have a terror of overacting. They consider it the cardinal sin. But underacting is just as false as overacting, and probably less gutsy. *Both* avoid experiencing what the character is supposed to be experiencing. It's just that one does it by showing off, the other does it by not showing up. But overacting is far more persecuted than underacting, and very few chronic underactors ever get called on it. Which is why I was so glad to read what two-time Oscar winner Gene Hackman had to say about it. He said that actors who underact do it to cover up their fear

> with a patina of being natural instead of being real. Real acting comes out of some kind of organic material you churn up in your soul or your body, and when you can't get to that, when you don't have time to get to that, you put a kind of patina of naturalism over it—which is death.

When you watch a scene class or an audition, you can always recognize the less-is-more actors: the first thing they do is reach for a chair to sit in during their monologue. Less-is-more actors love chairs. When they do a scene, they always position themselves face to face and very close to the other actor, which means the audience ends up only seeing one side of their face—like watching a coin do a scene instead of a person. When they speak, it is in hushed, almost conspiratorial tones, as if they were trying to make a sort of cocoon of earnest intimacy between themselves and the other actor.

The problem with this sort of acting in a theater is that not only does it seem cautious and weak, it actually looks more *unrealistic* than you might think. When people in real life are in the presence of someone they know (like characters in plays invariably are), they don't feel the need to force a physical intimacy by getting face to face with them and speaking quietly. In fact, when real people are with people they know they become a *fuller* version of themselves than they are in the presence of strangers, which makes them *speak more openly*. Notice the next time you talk with someone you *know* how loud the two of you are. People also *move more expansively* in a place they are familiar with than they do in public, where they curtail their personal energies. But in a place they know, people *expand* themselves *into the space* around them.

Someone once told Woody Allen during the rehearsal of a play he wrote that it was too long. Allen replied, "The play is not too long. The actors are too short." The point being that—even for a director who has gotten wonderfully subtle performances out of screen actors for years—sometimes less is just, disappointingly, *less*. Greatness doesn't get caught short.

## Dimension prevents cliché

One prime characteristic of great acting is that it is free of cliché. Cliché is a French word that was coined from the sound printing presses made as they clanged out copies: *cli-CHE, cli-CHE, cli-CHE*. So, at its root, cliché is a copy—something easy to manufacture and seen a zillion times before.

In acting, the most common form of cliché is *one-dimensional characterization*. Cliché characters come from thinking of a character as a limited set of "adjectives." Actors seize on a single, often obvious trait and give a performance that is one long variation on that single theme. Hamlet is "moody," Oscar Madison in *The Odd Couple* is "sloppy," Martha in *Who's Afraid of Virginia Woolf?* is "vulgar," Blanche DuBois is "delusional."

While this approach can work when you play lesser roles, or if you do a lot of TV work, it won't serve you if you want to play great roles—or play good roles in a way that rises to the level of greatness. F. Scott Fitzgerald said, "The mark of a first-rate mind is the ability to hold two opposing ideas at the same time and still retain the ability to function." Great characters *always* have first-rate minds: broken, vulnerable, even sometimes evil minds, but always first-rate.

Just as Fitzgerald said about great minds, great *characters* have opposing forces inside them that are locked in battle. Think, for example, of the great characters of our culture like James Dean and Marilyn Monroe—so great they still have a hold on our imaginations, decades after their deaths. (I mean, isn't every young, up-and-coming guy star a version of Dean and every girl a version of Monroe?) What makes these characters so fascinating is the opposing, and eternally unresolved, aspects of their natures. In Monroe it's the battle between *vixen* and *innocent*; in Dean it's between *thug* and *poet*.

Looking for these kinds of opposing qualities is the first step toward deepening your characterizations. Hamlet may be *moody*, but he also has a strong sense of justice. Oscar Madison may be *sloppy*, but he also likes Felix and wants him to be happy. Martha may be *vulgar*, but she also wants desperately to be admired. Blanche may be *delusional*, but she is also insightful.

The ongoing struggle between these forces will, like all battles, always be shifting slightly, with one side gaining the upper hand for a while and, then, vice versa. This constant, ever-changing movement will give your performance some nice fluctuations that will prevent cliché. And the more dynamic this internal battle between opposing forces, the greater your acting will seem to an audience.

## Don't sentimentalize

Sentimentality is the emotional version of cliché. Sentimentality is the fast food of emotion: it's franchised, commercial, and not very nourishing. It is real emotion, but emotion that is a dime-a-dozen. As the acting teacher Bobby Lewis joked, "If crying were acting, my Aunt Sadie would be Sarah Bernhardt."

Sentimentality can also be a dangerous cultural force, because the darkest hearts know how to use sentiment as a camouflage. (There was never a more intensely sentimental time or place than pre–World War II Germany.) The great American writer James Baldwin's biting comment on sentimentality nails it:

> Sentimentality, the ostentatious parading of excessive and spurious emotion, is the mark of dishonesty,

the inability to feel; the wet eyes of the sentimentalist betray his aversion to experience, his fear of life, his arid heart; and it is always, therefore, the signal of secret and violent inhumanity, the mask of cruelty.

Actors have a particular problem when it comes to avoiding sentiment. Because actors must expend so much *emotion* as part of their work, they are always struggling to regenerate it. So at times they will grab the handiest version of it, which is sentiment. But the better actors are honest with themselves and don't settle for cheap emotion.

You can always distinguish sentimental feeling from authentic emotion by two major characteristics. First, sentimental emotion is *all about the person who is feeling it*: sentimentalists are more interested in the fact that *they are feeling* than they are in *what* they are supposedly feeling.

Second, sentiment doesn't last. It feels bad the next day, its aftertaste is synthetic. As Hemingway expressed it in *The Sun Also Rises*: "Afterward, all that was faked turned bad and gave an unpleasant feeling."

See how you feel about your performance the next day. Any small wince of shame will let you know that you may be mistaking sentiment for deeper, truer, *greater* emotion.

## Go to the awkward

The best way for an actor to find more emotion is to *go to the awkward*.

Because the human brain's job is mainly to keep us functioning as a biological mechanism, it steers us away from feelings that might overwhelm us. Awkwardness and its awful "nails-on-a-chalkboard" sensation are an alarm the brain sends out to keep us from going into potentially flammable feelings; it's a kind of *Do Not Enter: High Voltage* sign.

It's one alarm that most people tend to obey. We will go to almost any length to avoid awkwardness. In its place we'll accept anger, sadness, even hatred rather than feel awkward. How many people go to their grave with an unspoken "I Love You" or apology on their lips, something never said for fear of simple awkwardness?

Anytime an actor tells me that he or she can't cry on stage or can't get angry or can't be intimate, a flag goes up for me. If you can't cry, it's not because you don't have enough feeling; it's because you have *so much* feeling that if you started crying you might not be able to stop.

Understanding this connection between awkwardness and emotion can be a big help to an actor. Where there is a conscious feeling of awkwardness, be assured that just beneath it in your subconscious is a wealth of strong emotion. For an actor, this awkwardness is like an "X" marked on a treasure map: it marks the spot where you should start digging for strong emotion. And great actors aren't afraid to get out the shovel.

## Great people have a feel for story

Most people that we think of as *great*—from any walk of life—have an innate understanding of story.

You can see it in great religious leaders, from Jesus to Gandhi to Martin Luther King, Jr.; in great political leaders, from FDR to Mandela; in great teachers, from Socrates to Joseph Campbell; even in great sportswriters, from Ring Lardner to Jim Murray.

If an actor is great, he or she can weave a compelling story out of *any* text. I once turned on the TV in the middle of a BBC documentary that was in mid-show. Richard Burton was giving an incredible performance of what seemed to be a poem. His presence was arresting, his eyes glistened with feeling, and he seemed deeply lost in the meaning of what he was saying. It all went something like this: Burton's eyes widening as he said slowly, "*I am,*" then, after a slight pause, "*You are.*" His voice started increasing in power as he said, "*He is. She is. THEY ARE!*" Then he looked as though he was hit by a jolt, took a breath, and said softly, "*We . . . are.*"

It turned out that he wasn't doing a poem at all. The interviewer had asked him a question about *Hamlet* and, as part of his answer, he was simply conjugating the verb "to be."

In the hands of a great actor a grammar exercise became a story—complete with a "he" and a "she" and a "they" and a "we" that seemed both so detailed in his mind and so full of meaning for him that it put you on the edge of your seat.

There is no surefire way to get better at being a "storyteller" as an actor, but you can bear in mind a couple of notions. *A feel for story is the ability to connect small details with larger meaning.* Henry James said, "A writer is someone on whom nothing is lost." It's a wonderful phrase. But he was talking about the *writer,* the teller of the tale and the explainer of their meaning. The actor, on the other hand, can't explain meaning, he or she has to *embody* it. The performance must show the audience how those small *details* connect to some larger *idea*.

I met a well-known actor, age ninety-four, who told me about the exact moment he committed to doing something "great with his life." In 1918, when he was *eight*, he accidentally broke the Victrola of his mean and abusive foster mother. She gave him such a thrashing that he vowed to become so "accomplished" in life that he would never have to endure that sort of shame again. And indeed he did do great things with his life.

But this moment from childhood had so seared itself into his mind that, when he got his first computer and e-mail account (at age ninety-two!), he chose for his password "Victrola 8."

One detail not only stayed in his mind for over eighty-some-odd years, it became, in a way, the story of his life. The preservation of that detail in his mind and heart, and his understanding of how it was a metaphor for his whole life, told me that this was a man who understood story. And thus a great actor.

Actors like this know how to take a detail and infuse it with meaning, just as they know how to give meaning (in the words of Shakespeare) "a local habitation and a name"—some sort of concrete manifestation.

Take Charlie Chaplin. In the hands of that actor, the sorry-looking little cane he carried became an element in a story. As the character of "The Tramp" used it, he seemed to be saying: "I may be down on my luck, but I still have enough delight in life to twirl my cane!" Because of the way Chaplin fleshed meaning into details, a simple gesture and prop become a story of human hope.

People who are good at *telling* stories are often good at *hearing* them. In the same way a good musician *feels* music more than a bad one, the first step to being able to *put something out* is the ability to *take it in* in the first place. As the Hasidic sages say, "Words that *come from* the heart, must first *enter* the heart."

Keep this in mind when you first read the script of any project you may work on. Your initial read is very important, because it is the only time you will be in the same position as your audience when they first see the story. So read it like a person. Don't read it like an actor, thinking the whole time, "Where are my lines and scenes?" Or "How's the director gonna pull off that effect?" Your original, "virginal" read will teach you all you need to know about the story, and you can draw on that experience as you prepare your role.

## Great actors don't have physical blocks

Eva Le Gallienne's book *The Mystic in the Theatre* is about the actress Eleonora Duse, who is acknowledged in world theater history as the most realistic actress ever, and arguably the greatest. Le Gallienne described the connection between *greatness* and the physical body of the actor.

> A great actor is not confined in the actual limits of the body. He is charged with an inner vitality that reaches out across the footlights to the farthest corners of the auditorium; it is almost tangible; it emanates from him, like an aura. When he stretches out his hand it is not the form of the hand that mat-

ters, but the vitality and rightness of the intention behind the gesture. This carries the hand beyond itself. In an inferior actor it stops at the end of the fingers which, instead of being open channels are dead ends.

Over the years of working with actors I have noticed that the really great ones have such a free flow of energy in their bodies that sometimes you can almost "see" it come off of them like sparks. But in other actors—less great actors—I notice that they often have one specific area of their body where the energy seems to "dead end," as Le Gallienne put it. A lot of them have one physical spot where they sort of "hold" on to themselves in a way that traps their flow of energy.

Over time I have found there are some *areas of the body at which many actors are commonly blocked*: the face, the throat, the upper chest, the stomach, and the groin. Whenever I explained this phenomenon to people, I had the habit of drawing a stick figure of a person and marking with Xs the spots on the body where these blocks tend to be.

Then a strange thing happened. Once, in a bookstore, the woman in front of me was checking out a book on Eastern religion. On the cover was a picture of a Hindu statue, and down the front of this figure's body were seven circles. These circles were marked in the exact same spots of the body that I marked when I drew sketches of actors' blocks.

Naturally I went and got a copy of the book, in which I learned about the concept of the *chakras*. This is the belief—a belief increasingly backed up by science—that there are seven energy centers in the body, and that these centers emit energy when they aren't *blocked.* Many people do exercises (yoga being the most popular) to "unblock" chakras and get a freer and healthy flow of energy.

Whatever the spiritual ramification of all this, I have found that when you ask actors to make a conscious effort to "open" whatever area of the body they are blocking off, you usually see a noticeable shift in their acting. Like unkinking a garden hose, something starts to flow better, and often the actors can access feelings they couldn't find when their energy was "dead-ending."

Great actors seem instinctively to align themselves in a way that allows them to get a flow of energy that makes for good acting. But an actor can also *develop* this ability. Try to notice those areas of your body that you seem to "protect" and hold on to. Make a conscious effort to open these areas, to allow the energy in them to be "exposed."

I once worked with an actress who always wore silk scarves. When working with her on a monologue, I asked her to take her scarf off. I was amazed (and so was she) at how much more vulnerable she became in her acting. It was a little scary for her, but wonderful.

## Don't shy away from the beauty of the carvings

"If you shield the mountain from the sandstorm, you will never know the beauty of the carvings."

These words of Elisabeth Kübler-Ross, author of the ground-breaking book *On Death and Dying*, were her way of explaining why she believed that the terminally ill patients she worked with looked "beautiful" to her, not horrifying as they looked to others.

Kübler-Ross felt that suffering, what she called "the sandstorm," carved away at a person's exterior until you could see his or her soul. This gave them (to use a Yeats phrase) "a terrible beauty" and a quality of stark *truth*.

*This idea of the "beauty of the carvings" is at the heart of greatness in acting.* The bottom line is that an actor must be able to suffer in public. That is what actors do. Plays and movies are not about people who are sheltered from storms; they are about people who are *in* the eye of the storm. The greater the actor you are, the more you allow the "sand storms" to carve into you— and the more courageously you show the beauty of your carvings to an audience.

Just a few months before she died, Jessica Tandy made an appearance at the Tony Awards. As she walked on stage, everyone in the audience could see the ravages of the cancer that would soon take her life. Tandy stood center stage, made herself taller and stronger and more luminous, the way that only a great actress can, and said, "I am grateful for the opportunity to step once more upon the stage." A writer from *Time* magazine described the moment:

> Like the boldest modern actress, this classically trained lady was daring the audience to be a party to *revelation*: look at me, see what's inside—the ache, the character, the beauty.

The great actors show people how beautiful honesty can be. Even painful honesty.

## Great performances shatter persona

American culture loves personas. Rooted in a dislike of ambiguity, as a society Americans like to put people into prefabricated categories or *personas*. (We *good*! They *bad*!) When people stray from their categories or "files" we've put them in—when their persona turns out to be different from the true face underneath it—America goes nuts. Nixon, OJ, Clinton, Michael Jackson—all the earthshaking American scandals have been about the "disconnect" between the person's projected persona and the reality of what he or she turned out to be.

Persona construction is a big part of our media, our advertising, and our politics. Beyond that, it has trickled down into the way individuals perceive themselves. People not only construct the persona they present to the world, they are reluctant to stray from it. Thus they wear the mask even when they're alone! (This is particularly true of young people, and doubly true of actors.)

The actress and teacher Anna Deavere Smith has said that some of the college students in her acting class are surprisingly reluctant to take off their jewelry or other signifiers of their persona in order to play a character in a scene.

But you cannot be a *great* actor if you won't let your persona drop or break. Great plays and movies are about the day that characters have their personas shattered. The critic Kenneth Tynan claimed that "an actor is a man who pretends to be someone who is pretending to be someone." In great plays we watch what "the man pretended to be" unravel. King Lear's persona as the head of his kingdom and household is shattered. In *Death of a Salesman*, Willy Loman's high opinion of himself and his son is shattered. In *Long Day's Journey into Night*, Mary Tyrone's pretense of being a loving and sober mother is shattered. Even in comedies, we laugh at the guy who gets hit with the pie because that indignity shatters his perfect persona.

*Drama is about what happens when a character is forced to stop playacting.*

The actor must be able to experience the shattering of persona. And that takes a measure of bravery. But great actors do it. They let both the persona of the character and their own persona fall away, in public. Those moments make for the most thrilling and memorable acting. The fall, the stripping, the shattering mask.

The very best description of it that I have ever found came from a Terrence Rafferty review of Sean Penn in *Dead Man Walking*.

> What makes his performance extraordinary is that Penn seems to be exploring the very nature of acting, examining the principles of his own art with a skeptical, self-critical eye, in order to transcend them. At the harrowing climax of "Dead Man Walking," both the actor and the character appear to have broken down utterly, and to have found in naked terror an odd sense of fulfillment—a release from the prison of performance.

That says it all.

## Deplete yourself

The difference between doing a "regular" role and doing a *great* role is that when you play the regular role it's possible to conserve your energy, hold back, not give

112 · *Notes to an Actor*

your all. Not so when you do great roles—the great roles won't let you.

Laurence Olivier, the actor who arguably gave more great performances of more great roles than anyone else in the twentieth century, described it this way:

> You are playing Othello, you give it all you've got. The author says to you, "You've given it all you've got? Good! You've done that? Fine. Now, more! More! M-O-R-E!" And your heart and your guts and your brain are pulp, and the part feeds on them. Acting great parts devours you. Great parts are cannibals.

An actress I knew was playing the lead in a production of *The Three Sisters*. When she played on Wednesday and Thursday she seemed to be conserving her energy, as if she were saving herself for the big Friday and Saturday performances and the always-full houses. A guy whom she was quasi-dating came into town and saw both the Wednesday and Thursday shows. Because she was aiming for him to remove the "quasi" from quasi-dating, she was determined to impress the hell out of him with her performance. So now she gave everything she had on Wednesday, and on Thursday she gave even more.

And then, she told me, she noticed something: her Friday and Saturday performances that week were even better. Depleting herself on Wednesday and Thursday didn't make her run out of gas for the weekend performances. It was as if a reserve tank of an even more interesting fuel kicked in after her regular tank had been emptied.

After that, she made it a point to try to give herself completely every night, to conserve nothing, even on the bluest-haired matinee performance. Not only did she find that her acting got better (some nights beyond better, to *great*), she found she was more able to hook into that thing we call "the creative state" when she was at the end of her strength.

Exhaustion shuts down our defenses. That's why interrogators have always used sleep deprivation to get prisoners to talk. When an actor reaches the point of depletion, he or she begins to lose that last bit of self-consciousness. That last door to the unconscious opens up, and whatever greatness is in there starts to flow.

Deplete yourself. Every time.

Just be aware that this depletion can affect you when you are offstage. When you are acting well it's as if all your doors are open—the doors to your mind and emotions, that is. In working up a performance, you learn to grease those hinges so they can open up when you need them to let the creativity flow in and raw feelings flow out. But occasionally these "doors" will either stay ajar after the show or will fly open unexpectedly at odd times offstage, in life.

Some of the symptoms of this "your doors are open" state are bone-crushing fatigue, anger (more fueled by adrenaline than real rage, but to loved ones it will seem like rage); volcanoes of inexplicable tears; and, finally, a tendency to lose things (car keys, wallets, important papers) and forget things like appointments and obligations—to say nothing of promises.

It's a normal part of doing good work and should be taken as a confirmation that the way you are working is the right way. You are tapping greater depths within yourself.

## *Great people don't have bad friends*

I sometimes think the reason people act is so they have something fascinating to talk about with friends in the bar after the show.

Acting and friendship have always gone hand in hand. Friends can have a profound effect on your development as a person, and as an actor. But the effect can, at times, be negative.

This is something people don't like to talk about. The self-help section of every bookstore is filled with titles about "dysfunctional" families and romances. Some books even advise how to relate better to your pet. But there's not one about the problem of having dysfunctional or toxic friends.

Actors in particular need to pay attention to the issue. Consider your friendships and be honest about whether they are contributing to your growth as a person and an artist, or dragging you down.

Toward that end, here are a few pointers. First, *never have untalented friends*. This is not to say that every friend has to be an actor or an artist. A friend's talent can be anything from gardening to raising children to playing the accordion. But talent needs to be around talent—and away from the passive-aggressive resentment of untalented people.

Second, your friends should not be an "audience" for you. Friends shouldn't be people for whom you need to put on a mask or play a character; they should be the people around whom you can throw off your mask, breathe free, and just *be*.

Third, misery doesn't love company; company loves misery—because it gives everyone something to talk about. But misery sucks. You should avoid it and avoid the people who thrive on it. Those wonderful friends who always love you when you *fail* may turn around and hate you when you *succeed*. Having that shoulder to cry on is comforting, but it is also addicting, especially for those who provide the shoulder, who may not want you to succeed for fear you will no longer need them. Beware.

## *If you fail, use it*

I once overheard someone in a bar say, "The way you handle your first broken heart can determine the course of your entire life." It's a scary thought, the idea that one failure could ruin you for so long a time. Whether or not it's true in love, I certainly think it's true in acting. Actors with potential who don't make the grade have—nine out of ten times—had a few early failures they weren't able to shake off.

All the acting books and acting classes in the world will never be as useful to you as the simple ability to *process failure*. When you are an actor, it is inevitable that failure will come, so you'll need a few tricks for disarming it.

First of all, when you fail, don't try to run away from the pain of it. Let yourself feel it for a few days—and feel it fully. According to Carl Jung, "neurosis is a substitute for *legitimate suffering*." In other words, if you don't allow yourself to feel the pain of something about which it's *legitimate* for you to feel suffering, those avoided feelings will come back to haunt you in odd and, according to Jung, *neurotic* ways. You'll become neurotic about your acting or about your career or about your "sense of self," and the skewed thinking of neurosis will cause you to make bad decisions, artistically and personally.

So if you should fail, give yourself a day or two to feel bad. Vent to friends, write maudlin things in your journal, give strangers the finger while driving. Feel the legitimate feelings. Do it for a pain-filled day or two. Then you will feel purged and ready for life again. Actors are always ready for something new, so after a few days of legitimate suffering you'll be free and open once again and ready to go back at it.

Second, when you experience failure and allow yourself to feel the pain of it, view it as a chance to experience a feeling you will be able to call upon in your acting. Plays and movies are not about people for whom everything is going just swell; they are about characters who are either in the throes of failing or struggling against the prospect of failing. This is true of every play from Oedipus, who fails to save his city from the curse of the Sphinx, to the guy in the farce who fails to keep his wife from finding the call girl in the linen closet.

*You cannot be a great actor unless you are able to feel failure in a real and passionate way on stage.*

When failure does come, use it. Try the following. Take a play off the shelf and act a scene or a monologue from it, trying consciously to use what you are feeling personally in your rendition of the character. Put your feelings to work. Doing this is no more bizarre than a jazz pianist sitting down to play the blues when he's sad. It's a good way to purge your feelings of sadness about what has gone wrong and at the same time remind you that you really aren't so bad an actor.

## *If you succeed, don't succumb to the Prometheus Syndrome*

Now, what of success? The fact is, as tough as failure may be, success can be even harder to contend with. Success is terrifying, and the scariest day of your life may be the day your dreams start coming true. A lot of actors just can't handle the vertigo of luck. They get caught up in what I call the "Prometheus Syndrome."

Prometheus was the character in Greek mythology who stole fire from the gods and gave that precious element to human beings. As punishment for doing this, he was chained to a rock for all eternity while eagles gnawed at his liver. (Clearly the gods don't like it when you steal their fire.)

When actors finally achieve success, they often succumb to the Prometheus Syndrome. They feel as if they've stolen fire from the gods and become fearful that some kind of divine retribution may be forthcoming. The next thing you know they are doing all sorts of self-destructive things to their careers (and their livers), long before the gods can lay a finger on them. All because of their Promethean terrors.

First and foremost, when success comes, *try not to self-mythologize.* In other words, resist the temptation to think of yourself and your career as a more important "drama" than the story of the characters you play. Don't put any creative energy into the construction of your own myth. In fact, stay away from myths altogether. As you can see from Prometheus's fate, characters in myths usually don't end up well!

And don't fall into the trap of believing that all talented people must be drawn toward drugs and booze. The assumption that talent and substance abuse must go hand in hand is an utter fallacy. For every talented actor or writer who is a drunk or a junkie, there are just as many alcoholic plumbers and addicted stockbrokers. We just hear more about the actors and writers because when they go into rehab it gets the kind of coverage in *People* magazine that no poor sap of a plumber ever gets. The assumption of a connection between talent and substance abuse is mistaken for what is really a connection between talent and publicity.

So set aside all those romanticized notions of self-destruction and concentrate on *becoming a better actor* and doing *good, soul-stirring projects*. The actors who stay interested in their art and work are the ones who have the staying power and weather success (like Robert De Niro, Tom Hanks, Nicole Kidman, Matthew Broderick).

## Greatness always has an undealt card

> *"There's something in their eyes that says, 'I know something you don't know.' And I wanted to be one of those kinds of performers."—Bob Dylan*

The great performers do seem to *know* something. They look as though they have a secret, something they know about themselves and about us, which they *could* tell us, but never do.

When you act, give your audience everything. But on stage *and* off be sure to reserve at least one card and never let them see it. Maintain a little mystery by always holding one undealt card.

Just make sure it's the *truest* card you have. That's what the greats do.

## Summary of Notes on Greatness

1. *To be great, you can't always need to be good.*
2. *Less isn't always more.*
3. *Dimension prevents cliché.*
4. *Don't sentimentalize.*
5. *Go to the awkward.*
6. *Great people have a feel for story.*
7. *Great actors don't have physical blocks.*
8. *Don't shy away from the beauty of the carvings.*
9. *Great performances shatter persona.*
10. *Deplete yourself.*
11. *Great people don't have bad friends.*
12. *If you fail, use it.*
13. *If you succeed, don't succumb to the Prometheus Syndrome.*
14. *Greatness always has an undealt card.*

# CHAPTER SIX

# COMEDY

## *Increase the contrast to increase the comedy*

While laughter is a single sensation, *comedy*, the force behind it, comes in many forms. Comedy embraces everything from elegant couples in a Noel Coward play, dangling martinis and swapping witty repartee, to the Three Stooges presiding over a donnybrook of flying pies. One quality, however, is present in all forms of comedy: *contrast*.

Two nuns get stuck in an elevator. Mildly funny. Turn the two people in the elevator into one *nun* and one *pimp* and now it's getting funnier. *Increase the contrast and you increase the humor.* Lose the contrast, there is no comedy. The pie has to hit the rich guy with the tuxedo and the toupee in order to be funny; the pie isn't funny if it hits the baker.

The actor who knows this little secret can always be on the lookout for the contrast in the material—the situation, the characters, the tone. And once you find the contrast, you'll have your most useful comic tool. Search out the dynamics of contrast in all the different guises of comedy, because it's there, in one form or another, in every comic dynamic.

The most enduring comic *plot*, for example, is to throw radically contrasting characters into the same situation. (That's why battling in-laws are such a solid sitcom mainstay. Whenever two or more in-laws are gathered, contrast will abound!) Situation comedies might just as easily be called *contrast* comedies, because all the situation does, essentially, is set up the contrasts.

Contrast is also at work in the way jokes are *structured*. Nine out of ten times the first part of the joke makes a 180-degree turn to contrast with the second half. Example:

*(Two ladies talking in a Boca Raton hair salon)*
Sadie: My husband Harold sent me flowers today.
   That means I'm gonna have to spend all night on
   my back with my legs spread.
Pearl: Why? Haven't you got a vase?

The first half of the joke sets you up for a discussion between Sadie and Pearl about sexual malaise, until Pearl takes things to an unexpectedly literal place. It's standard structure. Every joke is a surprise, and the surprise is simply a contrast between what you expect and what you get: part one, the "setup," contrasts with part two, the "punch line."

You will also find contrast at the heart of most comic *genres* and *forms*. *Farce* is about the contrast between anarchy and order. *Satire* and *parody* contrast reality with its exaggerated send-up. (You need to know George W. Bush to appreciate Will Ferrell's imitation.) *Camp* humor is (to use Susan Sontag's famous definition of it) "failed seriousness," something that is (again, Sontag) "so *good* because it is so *awful*"—a contrast between the tacky and the sublime.

*Puns* and *double entendres* are about contrasts in the meanings of words, like this famously raunchy opening-night telegram that humorist Dorothy Parker sent to an actor: *"A hand upon your opening. And may your parts grow bigger."* *Knock-knock jokes* contrast the answer to "Who's there?" with the answer to "Blankety-blank who?" Even *limericks* are a contrast between the lyrical first line "There once was a man from *Nantucket*" and the randy payoff line (in all the many possible rhymes for Nan-*tuck*-et). And of course, the most archetypal image of all, the *clown,* is a contrast between the graceful and the pathetic: threadbare tuxedo, crushed top hat, droopy lapel carnation.

All in all, the first rule of acting in comedy is: *Find the contrast in the material, and then figure out ways to use it.*

## Play against the "other"

"Smart" and "funny" have always been interdependent traits. Parents say "Don't get smart" or "Stop being a *wise* guy" to whichever one of their kids has the funniest comebacks. Chances are you will never meet a good comic who isn't also smart as a whip.

Comic actors have to be smart because comedy requires that an actor be able to *strategize.*

The "comic" needs to be *set up* in ways that the "dramatic" does not. When you act in comedy, you have to "position," so to speak, the elements of *contrast* because the humor will come from how you relate to whomever you are set in contrast to—what one might call *the other*, your partner in contrast: Ricky to Lucy, Laurel to Hardy, Archie to Edith.

At times the "other" can be a simple generic character, like Chaplin's Tramp versus *any cop*. The "other" can also be a group of people, like Benny Hill amid a gaggle of sexy ladies. Or it can be an object, like Buster Keaton versus the do-it-yourself, prefab house he tries to build, or Lucy versus the conveyor belt of candy. Whatever form the contrast takes, the good comic actor finds the smartest way to set his or her character in relation to "the other" for maximum contrast and thus maximum humor.

That's why many actors who were not especially funny in their early years can find a way to play a certain role that is hilarious—not because they are suddenly adopting a set of comic mannerisms or shtick, but because they *strategized* a way to work in contrast to the *other*. Examples would be Robert De Niro in recent movies like *Analyze This* and *Meet the Parents*. Or Leslie Nielsen, who was a square-jawed Hollywood leading man until he found a way to use his "manly seriousness" to great effect in a series of *Airplane* comedies. Or Candice Bergen, a leading lady and model who was so funny in her interaction with all the "others" in *Murphy Brown*.

It's not that these serious actors *became* funny in the way they sounded or moved or felt; they cleverly related to *others* in ways that created comic results.

When Walter Matthau played Oscar Madison in the original play and movie of Neil Simon's *The Odd Couple*, he didn't just do a lot of one-dimensional sloppy shtick. Everything he did in the film was in contrast to Jack Lemmon's prissy version of Felix Ungar. Matthau contrasted Lemmon's manic energy by playing Oscar with the offhanded, droopy quality of a jet-lagged basset hound, which contrasted hilariously with the high-strung Lemmon. Matthau and Lemmon increased the contrast by being good comic strategizers and ended up making comic history together.

Less clever actors not only don't find extra contrast in the material, they undermine the contrast that's plainly there. I once saw a regional theater production of *The Odd Couple* in which the actor playing Felix did so much over-the-top, palsied nervousness that in Act I he spilled some of a drink—something that the character, as written by Neil Simon, would *never* do. So when, in Act III, Felix is required to get upset when Oscar tosses a plate of spaghetti, I thought, "What are you so upset about? We all saw *you* spill a drink in Act I." The actor had failed to set up the proper contrast between the characters, and the play was not nearly as funny as it should have been.

## Stay in your lane

Drama is, I think, about "conflicts of love." Comedy is a little different. There will be some conflicts of love just as there are in drama, but comedy is also largely about *conflicts of thought*.

In "Who's on First?" Abbott thinks "Who" is the name of the first baseman. Costello thinks "Who" is a pronoun. And so it goes. A character is what a character *thinks about*: one person thinks of the fur as a luxurious garment, another thinks of it as a cute, fluffy animal's corpse. Our thoughts define us as characters. So when you act in comedy you need to project to the audience your character's thought process. To do this, you have to stay focused on what your character is thinking. And it's not as easy as it sounds.

When you do a comedy, you have to generate *double the amount of belief* that you need for a drama. Here's why. Comedy requires you to believe in things that are *ridiculous*, far more so than in drama. I mean, it's not hard for the dramatic actor to believe that Romeo would be distraught to see Juliet dead. It's a lot harder for an actor to believe that the bombastic performance Nick Bottom gives in *Pyrmus and Thisby* is really the brilliant performance that Bottom thinks it is. An actor must work extra hard to create credible belief in his or her character's perspective.

Otherwise you'll seem to be nudging the audience with your awareness of how ridiculous your character is. When you let us see your actor-awareness of the ridiculousness of your character's mind-set, you are condescending to the character. It's as if there's a scroll going across the bottom of your performance that keeps blinking: *"Isn't this character I'm playing ridiculous! And aren't I funny?!"*

The mark of the *great* comic actor is the ability to suspend judgment on the ridiculous things your character believes and to think as he thinks, without showing the audience the slightest sign that you are aware of their absurdity.

Here's a good way to think of it: always *stay in your lane* as a comic character—meaning, keep within your character's thought process and never veer into an awareness of the joke. That's for the audience to be aware of, not you.

Just *stay in your lane.*

Buster Keaton's face became the iconic face of comedy because, throughout all the chaos of the situations he got into—walls falling down around his ears, freight trains grazing his nose as they whiz by—Keaton's face maintained a look of vacant concentration on whatever task was at hand. He could be a Walker Evans photograph of a 1940s Midwest farmer mending a fence or a factory worker fixing an engine—just a guy, toiling away. Keaton was as locked in his lane as any laborer doing a good day's work, and it accounted for his genius and humanity.

Here's how you go about staying in your lane. Let's take another scene from *The Odd Couple.* On a hot New York night, Felix has crashed Oscar's poker game and made a halfhearted, melodramatic suicide attempt. The guys finally break up the game and leave Felix in the not-so-capable hands of Oscar. The following small scene involves Roy, Speed, and Vinnie, a henpecked accountant who is leaving in the morning for a trip to Florida. Here's the scene:

*(They all ad-lib goodbyes and leave. The door closes but opens immediately, and Roy comes back in.)*

Roy: (to Oscar) If anything happens, Oscar, just call me.

*(He exits, and as the door starts to close, it reopens and Speed comes in.)*

Speed: I'm three blocks away. I could be here in five minutes.

*(He exits, and as the door starts to close, it reopens and Vinnie comes back in.)*

Vinnie: If you need me I'll be at the Meridian Motel in Miami Beach.

Oscar: You'll be the first one I call, Vinnie.

Here's how an actor playing Vinnie might go about *not* staying in his lane. The actor could fall into the trap of playing generic comic agitation and worry over Felix, or play a veneer of nerdiness just because the character is a henpecked accountant, or do a piece of physical shtick as he goes in and out the door. But if the actor wants to stay in Vinnie's lane, he should be *thinking* something like this:

*There's a very good chance that Oscar will call me if Felix has a problem because I am superb in a crisis, like that time I had to do the Heimlich maneuver on the rabbi at my nephew's bar mitzvah. So when I get to Florida I have to be sure to tell all the people in the hotel to come out and find me by the pool if they get a call at the front desk that "an Oscar Madison left a message saying, 'Please get Vinnie! I need Vinnie! Dependable, smart, strong, heroic VINNIE! I WANT VINNIE!!!' Poor Oscar, what will he do without me?!*

The actor should believe every word of this, down to his toes. He should leave that game feeling every bit the hero he may be called upon to be if Oscar can't handle Felix without him. That would be staying in his lane.

## Intensify the focus on obsession and oblivion

As I have said, when you're clear about the comic patterns at work in a scene, you'll be able to strategize ways that your character can fit into the dynamic. These next three notes are about some of the common *patterns of contrast* to look for.

One pattern is the *obsessive* character versus the *oblivious* character. The obsessive character is so fixated on some irrational goal that he is blind to the effects of his actions. This applies to anything from Lucy's crazy schemes to break into show business to the characters in *A Midsummer Night's Dream,* drugged on a magic love potion, who fall head-over-heels in love with the wrong people.

Obsession versus oblivion is, in a sense, the comic version of the most basic tragic plot. There are countless dramas about obsessed characters who are oblivious of where their compulsions will lead them (Oedipus, Lear, Willy Loman). This tragic pattern becomes comic when the obsessed person is after something that the audience knows is utterly *absurd*. About Lucy we think, "What the heck is the big deal about performing at the Tropicana, for heaven's sake?" The audience's awareness that the character's "object of obsession" is such a silly thing saves it from being "too dark" for them to laugh at. If Lucy were always plotting with Ethel to find ways of committing adultery or scoring drugs instead of getting into a show, the audience wouldn't feel as free to laugh.

When you play the role of a comically obsessed character, take into account that since the audience *knows* the object of your obsession is absurd, you can and should play the obsession with *real feeling* and *compulsive seriousness*. Make the audience believe that *you* are obsessed down to your toes.

A current master of this sort of comedy is Lewis Black, a stand-up comedian who has turned the "angry rant" into comic art. Black doesn't give you any sense that he has spent hours sitting in a room carefully crafting jokes. He looks like he has been up all night pacing the floor, tortured by the things he rails about (outlandish prices for bottled water, or finding too many different kinds of milk in the store). He never lets you know that the obsession is really a well-honed comic technique. He plays it like a man possessed—and he never lets you see the chink in his straitjacket.

Another common comic dynamic is the pairing of an obsessive character with someone who has no clue about this person's crazy schemes and notions: someone who is *oblivious*. It's only at the climax of the story, when the obsessive character becomes "unplugged," that the clueless is shocked out of his oblivion. A classic example is Ricky Ricardo singing three-quarters of a Cuban love song unaware that his wife—who is sloshed on Vita-meat-a-veg-a-min—is sharing the stage with him. He sings away oblivious to her machinations until she finally pounces. Only then does he become aware—and unglued.

The key to playing the oblivious character is to realize that oblivion doesn't come from thinking about nothing, and it doesn't come from cluelessness. It comes from the character thinking very hard about something—something *wrong*! Ricky is going at that song with such earnest concentration and gusto that the contrast between his oblivion and Lucy's obsession makes for a comic dynamic that people still discuss fifty years after the show first aired.

Remember that comic obsession and comic obliviousness are both born of the same thing: hyperfocus.

## Heat up "hot" characters, cool down "cool" ones

The concept of *hot* and *cool* characters comes from Marshall McLuhan, the media critic who coined the phrase "global village." McLuhan believed there are two types of characters, "cool" and "hot." Cool characters personify *normalcy*: they have basic common sense and a solid grasp on reality. Audiences tend to identify with cool characters since most people view themselves as "normal."

Hot characters, on the other hand, represent *oddity*: they are unusual, they have idiosyncrasies and skewed perceptions of reality. Audiences love these characters but don't identify with them, so they prefer to take these characters in limited doses. For example, you could watch the cool, easy "normal-guy" quality of Jay Leno every night; but the hotter Bill Maher fares better once a week.

If you look at just about any sitcom you will see this hot-cool dynamic at work. The *main* character is often the cool one: Jerry Seinfeld, Mary Tyler Moore, Candice

Bergen in *Murphy Brown*, Ray Romano in *Everybody Loves Raymond*. These cooler characters maintain a perspective of amused normalcy as an array of *hot* characters orbit around them—hot characters like Kramer in *Seinfeld*, Ted Baxter in *The Mary Tyler Moore Show*, Elden the Housepainter in *Murphy Brown,* or the entire family in *Everybody Loves Raymond.*

Hot and cool characters depend utterly on each other, because they feed off the contrasts between them. If the contrast between their coolness and hotness isn't extreme enough, there's no humor. This is why so many spin-offs of successful sitcoms fail. A hot character from a hit show is given his own show, and the audience just can't take a full blast of such a hot character. More commonly, though, the producers of the new show try to cool down the once-hot character, making the character less funny than he or she was in the context of the original show, where the hot-cool dynamic was in perfect sync.

Once you grasp the concept of hot and cool characters, it should be easy to figure out which type your character is, since they are usually one or the other. But you will face a more challenging situation when your character is not fixed as hot or cool but fluctuates between both.

Every one of the lead characters on *Friends* is an example of this, all six of them. Each one could and did play *both* hot and cool. Whoever was crazed in love, guy or girl, would be in *hot* mode—irrational and totally bonkers—while the saner "sounding board" friend they confer with stays in *cool* mode. With the plot reshuffled for another episode, last week's hot and cool would reverse their comic functions.

(I think one of the reasons *Friends* ran for ten successful years was because of the endless comic possibilities presented when an entire cast of characters is able to keep switching off between hot and cool. I can't name another sitcom for which this was true. Producers, take note!)

Understanding this hot-cool dynamic will help you avoid some basic mistakes made in handling comic material. One of the most common is when an actor who should be playing the *cool* character becomes too *hot*. This usually happens because the actor playing the cool character gets freaked out (consciously or otherwise) when the hot character seems to be getting all the laughs. (That may very well be the case; but the laughs that the hot character gets depend on the cool character as a bouncing ball depends on the surface it hits against for its bounce.) Whenever the actor playing the cool character starts heating up by "trying to be funny," the contrast slacks off and the scene is not as funny.

This is the problem with most bad sitcoms. Everyone tries to be a hot character by adopting some shticky manner. But no one has the comic know-how to be cool and allow a hotter character to hit off them to get the comic bounce going.

Two hots don't make a funny. What would Lucy have been if Ricky had been played by Red Skelton? All mice, no cat. Too hot, and not as funny.

## Sustain the tension of the bursting point

Something is always getting ready to *burst* in comedy. The word "comedy" comes from the Greek word *comus*.

A comus was a folk ritual, performed in ancient Athens, in which the dancing participants wore enormous *erect phalluses* strapped to their bodies. (Oh those nutty Greeks!)

This was a theatrical depiction of a very basic comic construct. People have always found humor in the tension between an expanding *life-force* and some *force of containment*. The phallus is a metaphoric image of swelling "life" being "contained"—in this case by a grotesquely anguished body part that's ready to burst.

In *slapstick* that tension can be physical anarchy: the Three Stooges as wallpaper hangers, versus the elegant society lady who is trying to host a fancy garden party. In *character comedy* it's when one character functions as a wild force of nature and one as its container, like Harry trying to get Sally to stop having a fake orgasm in a crowded deli. In *farce* (a word that comes from an Italian word for "stuffing"—note the similarity to "bursting"), it's the way that chaotic events swell against some force of order: the ship's captain trying to contain the Marx Brothers.

For actors, the key to getting this comic dynamic right is to be sure you know whether your character is functioning as the life-force (Lucy) or the container (Ricky). Next, it's vital that you *sustain the tension between the two forces*. If you let it go for even a second, it is like one side letting go in a tug-of-war—it falls apart. To put it in *I Love Lucy* terms, no actor should ever slow down the conveyor belt of candy. No comic actor should ever let go of the comic tension to show off on his or her own. (It's so destructive to the comic dynamics of the play that Shakespeare, in his "advice to the players" said he would have such a fellow *whipped*. He then goes on to compare him to Herod, the biblical king known for slaughtering children. Now that's a note to an actor!)

But Shakespeare had a point. For a comic to care more about his or her own characterization rather than in maintaining this all-important comic tension between *life-force* and *container* is like a percussionist in a symphony that's doing the *1812 Overture* deciding that he's going to hit the cymbal when he wants to, rather than at the high-tension point the piece has been building up to. That musician-like awareness of maintaining tension should be part of your comic arsenal.

## It's okay to be "over the top" if you have a bottom

There have been many famous "larger-than-life" characterizations in the history of comedy: Jackie Gleason in *The Honeymooners*, Lucille Ball in *I Love Lucy*, Zero Mostel in *The Producers*, Gene Wilder in *Young Frankenstein*, Bill Murray in *Caddyshack*, Jim Carrey in *Ace Ventura*. While all these performances have a "size" that we might affectionately call *over the top*, their brilliance comes from how deeply *the actor feels the actual emotion* of the character.

The feeling that goes into a great comic performance has as much reality and heart as any actor would need to do Shakespearean tragedy. At times the rage that Gleason's Ralph Kramden directs toward Norton has the force of King Lear. Carrey's Ace Ventura has some of Mark Anthony's impassioned righteousness. Lucy stuffs chocolates down her blouse with the mounting panic of a Lady Macbeth trying to rub out her "damned spot."

While great comic actors may indeed use the fuel of emotion to light a bonfire of exaggeration in their characterization, their emotion is real and deep.

*Resist the temptation to think of broad comedy as having false emotion.*

What makes something funny is the fullness and authenticity of an emotion, contrasted with *the absurdity* of what is causing the emotion in the character. Understanding this is, I think, the dividing line between good and great in comedy. *Great comic actors feel the emotions of their characters more fully than merely good comic actors do.* Maybe this is why so many comic actors have also excelled in purely dramatic roles (Gleason, George Burns, and Carol Burnett come to mind, and Robin Williams—who, remember, won his Oscar for a dramatic role).

It's fine for you to create a character who is over the top as long as that character has *a bottom*—a bottom of truthful emotion.

## Be extra precise in comedy

Always try to get the *uncontrollable* laugh, not the laugh that says, "I should laugh at this, it's the thing to do." I'm talking about the magic one, the one you can't control, the one that comes with what we call *stitches* and makes you feel like you're being torn apart by your own laughter. (Not a bad way to go.)

This sort of laugh comes from the sense of *perfect precision* you get when the whole universe and the laws of physics themselves seem to be in on the joke. The chubby neighbor has to walk into the yard at the *exact moment* the Frisbee flies to the gateway and hits him in the face for everyone at the pool party to laugh uncontrollably. A millisecond too early or late and it's not perfect. You get laughter but not *stitches*. Grandpa leans in to blow out the candles on the cake with all the loved ones counting One! Two! Three! But on "three" the only thing he blows is a fart. The family convulses. If he farts on "one," not as precise, not as funny.

And it's not just about the perfectly precise physical circumstances: the characters must be perfect as well. Like the time I saw a Yuppie couple in New York's Central Park having an argument on the bench next to me. (Not an argument so much as the guy doing a monologue about how wonderful he was compared to her.) I frankly thought he was a jerk, and obviously so did the bird who decided to fly over and crap on him, and do so at just the right moment: splat! Right onto the guy's eyeglasses (glasses tend to make everything funnier).

You need precision if you want those stitches.

Buster Keaton was a master of comic precision. If you've ever seen footage of him explaining how to "take a pie," you'll know what I mean. ("Taking a pie" is a maneuver that entails turning around a *split second* before being greeted in the face by a flying pie.) No one took one better or more precisely. It's probably no small coincidence that this great master of comic precision was also something of an amateur engineer who spent his (rather sad and boozy) declining years on his San Fernando Valley ranch, making elaborate model train rails on which little locomotives would do things on request, like chug over to your chair and light your cigarette.

Even after the comedy stopped, the precision remained.

"Exact instants" and "split seconds" aren't so much the stuff of drama, but comedy loves them, because it thrives on precision in ways that drama doesn't need to. You can cry anytime you want in a scene from *Medea*, but you have to get hit in the face with the door at *just the right moment* in the farce *Noises Off*. And you can tell a sad story any number of ways and never be accused of "not telling it right," but funny stories or jokes can fall apart because of imprecision. We all have annoying relatives who tell jokes like this: "*A rabbi and a hooker walk into a bar . . .* no wait, sorry . . . I mean *a rabbi and a bartender walk into a brothel . . .* oops, no, that's wrong. . . . *A bartender and a hooker walk into a synagogue . . .* etc."

The need for precision in comedy even carries over into specific *words*. All good comic writers know that the punch and rhythm of a funny line can be damaged, or at least lessened, because of a few harmless words being out of place or misspoken. If instead of correctly saying Woody Allen's famous quip "It's not that I'm afraid to die. I just don't want to be there when it happens," you said, "It's not that I'm afraid of death. I just don't want to be there when it happens," it's less funny. "Death" is an abstract idea whereas "to die" is a verb—active and funnier. Or if you said, "I'm not afraid to die. I just don't want to be there when it happens," we would miss the beginning part, the "It's not that . . ." It's a better way to begin the phrase because the relaxed, confident tone of "It's not that I'm afraid to die . . ." will be a better contrast to the irrational, terror-driven pay-off line.

When you act in a comedy—especially one by a good comic writer like Allen or Simon or Mel Brooks—get the words exactly right. It matters. The audience will notice on a subliminal level, and the writer will really notice and appreciate it. Because as Mark Twain, the best humorist ever, once said, "The difference between the *almost*-right word and the right word is really the difference between the lightning bug and the lightning."

## Use active contrast to create comic timing

Ask actors to tell you what they consider the most important skill for playing comedy and they are likely to say the same thing: *timing*. But if you then ask them to explain exactly *what* comic timing is, they will have trouble doing so.

We know comic timing when we see it, but what it takes to actually do it well is elusive.

One of the best teachers of comic timing ever was the great Broadway director George Abbott. By the time he died (at the age of 106!) he was regarded as the Obi-Wan Kenobi of comic timing. Every actor who was directed by him has at least one piece of George Abbott advice they never forgot. He was legendary for telling actors things like: "Hang up the phone, freeze for a beat, turn quickly, and say the line loud."

While some actors balked at his absurdly specific orders, most found that if they did what he told them to do on stage, sure enough they'd get a bigger laugh.

There is a theme to most of the pointers Abbott gave actors about comic timing. Much of it centered on getting them *not* to make the smooth, gradual transitions one would in drama. Instead Abbott had the actor sort of "jump" from one mode of energy to a different mode of energy, with almost *no transition*. When the actor *did* "hang up the phone, *freeze* for a beat, *turn quickly,* and say the line loud," the *movement* and *thud* of hanging up the phone would jump to *stillness* and *silence* for the "freeze" and jump again to *movement* and *volume* of "turn quickly and say the line loud."

When the energy of one moment directly contrasts with the energy of the next moment, people find it innately funny. (Once you've been stuck playing peekaboo with the toddler in the seat in front of you on the plane, you'll see just how innate.)

This is why it's so funny to watch film footage in *fast-forward*. Something primal in us finds it hilarious. Show a group of people any video in fast-forward and, even if it's footage of a serious event—a football game, a wedding, a funeral cortege—it can reduce a roomful of mature adults to giggling fools.

In fast-forward there *are no normal transitions* because they go by too quickly to be perceived. They seem to *jump* from one moment to the next, creating a contrast from moment to moment: bride kneels, bride stands, bride kneels, then stands, they kiss, etc. With the natural transitions fast-forwarded out, it's a scream.

Here are two good examples of the notion that timing is contrast in action. First, any improvisational riff done by Robin Williams. It's not so much the *quality* of what he does as it is the sheer *quantity* of the contrasts in energy he gives you. He goes from imitating Arnold Schwarzenegger to a swishy interior decorator to someone with Tourette's syndrome, all in a matter of milliseconds. People laugh at what we may think of as masterful timing but what is in reality a rapid-firing series of *contrasting* energies.

Another good example are the classic Looney Tunes cartoons like Bugs Bunny and Road Runner. These could be watched as master classes in timing, in their use of contrast in action and sound. Here's what happens when Wile E. Coyote, in frantic pursuit of the Road Runner, mistakenly runs off a cliff: a moment of stillness in midair when he realizes he has gone too far, then silence, then a feeble glance up to the camera that seems to say "Oh shit!", then a split-second pause—stillness. Then, with no warning, a fast, harrowing plunge and the fading whoosh of a falling fool. Then silence. Then the sound of a "thud" and a small puff of dirt at the bottom of a canyon. Voilà! Virtuosity of contrast in action and sound. Each segment of the sequence clean and clear, each moment in sharp contrast with the previous moment.

Making these "nontransition transitions" is no easy thing for an actor to do. It takes virtuosity and practice to execute this technique sharply and have it seem natural. These "jumps" require a physical dexterity and, even more important, a good musical ear, which may be why many great comic talents also excel at music. Woody Allen plays clarinet in a jazz band. Johnny Carson was a skilled drummer, as is Dana Carvey. Jack Lemmon and Art Carney were both good pianists who played by ear. Danny Kaye and Jackie Gleason conducted orchestras. Charlie Chaplin wrote the music for his movies. Mel Brooks won a Tony Award for the score of *The Producers*. Sid Caesar plays the saxophone. Jack Benny played the violin better than he pretended. David Hyde Pierce is an excellent classical pianist.

If you are aware of these technical aspects of timing and combine them with your own instinct about what's funny, your comic timing is bound to improve. And if you need models for this notion that *timing is contrast in action and sound*, listen to the way Robin Williams or Nathan Lane make vocal transitions, or study the lightning-fast physical transitions of Charlie Chaplin or Jim Carrey. And for *both* vocal and physical virtuosity, of course, watch Lucy.

## Don't move from one moment to the next without establishing

*Sloppiness*, which is the hallmark of the comic amateur, is rarely funny—at least not "stitches" funny.

The imprecision and sluggish timing that can weaken comedy is caused by allowing the energy that's generated during a comic performance to cause you to grow *sloppy*. The most common version of comic sloppiness is the failure to let one moment *establish* itself before moving on to the next one.

This note is similar to an earlier note in this book in the chapter on Talent, the one about "talented actors don't skip notes." That's another way of saying, "Let moments establish." But there are refinements on this idea that can help with comedy in particular.

The moments or beats that must be established in comedy are shorter than they are in drama. Hilarity tends to grow out of a *series* of actions—actions that *escalate*, one step at a time, until they reach their height. Each one of these actions, each one of these steps in the series, must be *established*, meaning that you must be sure the audience has fully perceived it before you can move to the next action/step. If you allow performance energy to make you sloppy, you will blur one moment into the next before it can fully register with the audience. Steps will be missed, beats will blur together, and you will not get those sharp contrasts between moments that escalate into stitches-funny.

For an example of masterful establishing, watch the episode of *I Love Lucy* where Lucy puts on a long, putty nose to disguise herself from William Holden. Here is one small moment of that famous scene, written out step by step.

1. Holden stares curiously at Lucy's strange nose.
2. She "takes in" Holden staring at her nose. This makes her nervous about her disguise.
3. She starts to fiddle self-consciously with her fake nose. In her nervousness, she bends it so that it is now crooked.
4. Lucy crosses her eyes to look in panic at the skewed nose.
5. Holden and Ricky react in horror.
6. Lucy sees their reaction, and it makes her even more nervous.
7. She tries to compensate by pushing the nose back into shape, but this only makes it worse. The nose is now hopelessly mashed.
8. Lucy looks down at her nose half in horror, half trying to act nonchalant—as if to say, "I hate when this happens."

9. Holden and Ricky look with complete shock at the surreal angle of Lucy's ruined nose.
10. Lucy sees them react and gets even more panicked.

If you are an actor who doesn't *establish*, you won't go through *ten* steps, like Lucy does—you'll only have, maybe, five. As a result, it will be only half as funny, the hilarity reaching only half as high. So learn from Lucy and let *each* moment establish clearly.

An actress friend once told me about the time Lucille Ball came to her college to talk to the theater students. It was very late in Lucy's life and, according to my friend, she seemed a little feeble. For the entire class she mainly just kept saying two words, over and over again: *"Act!"* and *"React!"* All day long: *"Act!"* and *"React!"* Kids would do a scene and she'd bellow, "No! No! No! You're supposed to *Act!* and *React!*"

It was an awkward afternoon of an elderly legend doing her best to drive home a point to a bunch of unimpressed and no doubt passively rude students. It even became a bit of a joke within the school, with the theater students always saying to each other "Act! and React! Ha Ha!"

It's a sad story. Not for Lucy, but sad that the students thought her advice was silly and did not realize she was handing them one of the great secrets of acting in comedy—perhaps Ball's greatest skill as a comedienne. By saying *act* and *react*, I believe she was saying, "Let the moments establish." Look again at the above steps of the gag. You'll notice that between every *act*ion there is a *react*ion: a moment of establishment, a chance for each comic moment to make its impact.

Just like a great prizefighter making sure every punch lands squarely until his opponent is flattened, Lucy made sure each comic moment landed squarely until she destroyed an audience with laughter.

So be sure to let the moments establish. Or, in the words of a master, "Act and react!"

## Play character, not energy

Comedy loves a crowd. We call people into the room for something funny on TV, not for something sad. We laugh if we fall off a chair at the office party, but not if we fall off with no one around. This natural symbiosis between crowds and laughter affects the relationship between an actor and an audience.

Tell an actor that you saw him or her in a comedy and the first thing they say is "Really? *What night?*" Actors always remember which were the good ones and which were the duds. And you can't blame them. The actor/audience relationship is more active and interdependent with comedy than it is with drama. When a comedy isn't going well, it's painfully obvious. *Not laughing* equals *show not going well*, whereas actors in a drama giving a performance in front of a dead house can always console themselves with that old standby, "I think they're really listening."

But oversensitivity to the audience can make a comic actor become more fixated on getting a response from the crowd than on living the life of the character. The moment some actors hit the stage in a comedy their goal is to "get laughs." And if they don't get them in the early part of the performance, they panic and start begging for them by *pushing*.

The mistake here is expecting an audience to laugh before they have gotten to know the characters. People can't laugh at someone they don't *know*. If I tell you that Person A tried to kiss Person B, you won't necessarily find that amusing, unless I tell you that Person A was *Little Richard* and Person B was *Reverend Jerry Falwell*. Then you laugh, because your *knowledge of these "characters"* makes it funny. It's why families have so many inside jokes that nonfamily members don't understand. Others don't have the privilege of knowing "that trick Uncle Al does with his false teeth after he's had one too many daiquiris."

*Your primary concern in the early part of a performance should not be to get laughs at all costs. It should be to let the audience get to know your character and your character's thought process.*

Noel Coward's motto for relating to audiences in a comedy was "Throw 'em away in the first act, pull 'em back in the second act." That's a good way to think about it; don't worry about reeling in the audience with the big laughs until you make sure they know all the components that will pay off in the comic climaxes.

Thinking this way will prevent you from falling into the biggest trap of all in playing comedy, which is trying to get laughs by exerting a generic brand of comic pep. It's amazing how many actors do this. They hear "comedy" and immediately start revving up this synthetic energy. Then they hit the stage like they've had one too many Red Bulls.

*Trying to get laughs by being "energetic" is like trying to make your writing funnier by adding exclamation points.*

Energy will come from *character*, but character won't come from *forced energy*. Trust the audience to laugh once they get to know your character's truth—and then see that you play it truthfully.

Director Mike Nichols nailed the difference between actors who let the truth of character do the work and those who try to force it with an overwrought energy. He said, "I noticed long ago that there are two kinds of actors. There's the kind who get a little bit encrusted as time goes on. And there's the kind that get a little truer, about 4 percent truer every night."

When you play comedy there will, of course, be some magical performances when the audience is simply "with you," where you "can do no wrong," where every move you make gets a laugh. Those wonderful nights take care of themselves. It's the rockier ones you'll need a strategy for handling. The best comment I ever heard about audiences at a comedy came from Matthew Broderick: "When they are with me, I include them, and when they aren't, I don't."

That's an excellent strategy for dealing with an audience. When they are with you, *let them in,* or as Coward said, "Pull them back." But if they aren't quite with you, don't go after them. Just be more real, *be more of the character*, be 4 percent truer.

One final note about audiences at comedies: even bad audiences don't know they're bad. I've never heard someone coming out of a comedy say, "Gee, we were an awful audience." Audiences always think they're great.

They'll only know they're a bad audience if you treat them like they are. So don't.

## Comedy is tragedy without dignity

When someone in real life experiences a tragedy, the people around him treat the suffering person very well. It's as if the Fates had marked the sufferer as "special." Tragedy has a way of conferring dignity on people. "The poor, brave widow," etc. Comedy, on the other hand, yanks all dignity right out from under you.

If there is no loss of dignity, there is no comedy. In comedy either someone else's dignity is being taken away by the comic, as when Bill Maher or Dennis Miller skewers people; or people are willingly relinquishing their own dignity for a laugh: Chris Farley, Phyllis Diller, John Belushi. Either way it can be a harsh endeavor, because while comedy can support as much pain as tragedy, it must be endured without the "Novocain" of dignity that helps people get through tragedies.

*Comedy is tragedy without dignity.*

And that can wear on you. The tragic clown has always been a cliché. People assume it's the sad person who gets *drawn* to comedy as a way of dealing with or escaping his sadness. But I also think a case can be made that doing comedy can *make* a person sadder because of the loss of dignity that is comedy's great occupational hazard. Comedy exacts a cost.

Comic actors must either be cruel enough to *take* away someone else's dignity or masochistic enough to *give* away their own.

The English comedian Benny Hill was known for his bawdy TV show in which he spent most of his time in hilarious pursuit of buxom women. He was a very funny man, but when I read the following obituary, it made me sad.

> Despite his wealth, he was known to ride buses and quietly arrange to take disabled people on outings. He was a lifelong bachelor; his biography says two women rejected his marriage proposals many years ago. In a rare personal comment Hill recently said, "To be in love with someone who doesn't love you back gives you a pain in the chest at night." There were no known survivors.

I got the sense that Hill would have traded a few of the millions of laughs he got for the basic dignity that comes when someone you love loves you back.

It's why great comics are, I think, so brave. Half the world feels "that pain in the chest at night," but only a gifted few have the guts and know-how to weave the broken heart into hilarity.

Stitches indeed.

---

## Summary of Notes on Comedy

1. *Increase the contrast to increase the comedy.*
2. *Play against the "other."*
3. *Stay in your lane.*
4. *Intensify the focus on obsession and oblivion.*
5. *Heat up "hot" characters, cool down "cool" ones.*
6. *Sustain the tension of the bursting point.*

7. *It's okay to be over the top if you have a bottom.*
8. *Be extra precise in comedy.*
9. *Use active contrast to create comic timing.*
10. *Don't move from one moment to the next without establishing.*
11. *Play character, not energy.*
12. *Comedy is tragedy without dignity.*

CHAPTER SEVEN

# SHAKESPEARE

*Don't be intimidated because you are American*

When asked to name who he thought was the "greatest living American playwright," the provocative director Peter Sellars replied without hesitation, "Shakespeare."

I agree. There is so much in the work of Shakespeare that captures the energies of America that he could be "ours." The moxie of his characters, their desire to "be somebody," their sense that greatness lies not where they *are* but in a far-off "fantasy and trick of *fame*," as Hamlet says, is all, to my mind very American.

Unfortunately, Americans—actors and nonactors— have always been intimidated by Shakespeare. Especially when it comes to our deference to the British: we seem to think they have cornered the market on the Bard. But, ironically, the Brits don't feel this way at all about us. Many of them scratch their heads in wonderment at the American reluctance to do Shakespeare.

They know we could be damn good at it. As the famed British director Peter Hall put it:

> Americans have been going down on one knee before the God of Shakespeare, when they possess all the skills of dynamic language and physicality—speed, wit, naturalism, daring—to burst through the conventions and make them new. If they could learn to observe the form and breathe in the right places, *they'd kick the shit out of us!*

So why aren't we "kicking the shit" out of the Brits when it comes to Shakespeare, the way that Hall and other Brits are beckoning us to?

Part of the reason, I think, has to do with the way Americans are first exposed to Shakespeare as opposed to the way the Brits are. A British kid's first encounter with Shakespeare is usually *in a theater*—where his plays belong. There a kid can be thrilled by the spectacle—the battles, the colors, the songs, the crowds, the costumes, and the noise—all the wonder of Shakespeare's plays in performance.

An American kid's first encounter with Shakespeare tends to be in some drab English class, sitting at a hard desk, in a roomful of bored faces all staring into big books. A very untheatrical setting. And to make matters worse, the first person to expose American kids to Shakespeare is often a moldy literature teacher, either Mr. McGeek, who wouldn't know what to do with a sword if one poked him in the ass, or Miss Frowsy, whom no man in his right mind would climb a balcony to kiss goodnight.

Many American actors avoid Shakespeare because they are intimidated by him. But I think they are intimidated *because they avoid him.* Once actors are exposed to him, they find great roles, of course, but they also find the greatest acting teacher or acting class there is. I have never seen an American actor who did a major role in a Shakespeare play who didn't emerge from the experience a changed person and twice the actor as before.

American actors should make Shakespeare their own. That doesn't mean I advocate those hackneyed productions that do things like set Shakespeare in a cowboy town. ("A plague on both your wagon trains!") No. Nor do you have to do Shakespeare with a deliberate Brooklyn accent or a Southern drawl. It just means that you look in the play for *thematic actions* that you and your audience can relate to. And they are there.

Shakespeare's plays are about characters who want "to be" something or be someone more than they are. Often the dramatic action of the story is the progress they make toward transforming their identities, for better or worse. Hamlet starts out as his father's immobilized orphan and ends up as his avenger; Juliet begins as the dutiful daughter of Lord Capulet and ends as the daring wife of her lover Romeo. At times the characters' transformations are so great they actually change their names: war hero Henry V starts out as rowdy Hal; the ambitious Earl of Gloucester ends up as the dangerous King Richard III; Macbeth is called Thane of Cawdor by the witches even before he assumes the name that will carry him into tragedy. In the dramas the transformations happen by means of political and social machinations; in the comedies the transformation happens by means of trips to magical woods and love potions.

Either way, everyone seems to be asking "to be or not to be," and everyone is engaged in the business of "becoming." This is, in my opinion, the central energy of Shakespeare's plays, and it happens to be a very American energy as well. We Americans want to believe that what we are today is not as great as what we may become tomorrow. As Willy Loman says in *Death of a Salesman,* "A man can't go out the way he came in. . . . A man's got to add up to something." Americans feel the burden of adding up to something. Americans have the itch to—in the words of *On the Waterfront*'s Terry Malloy, "be a contender." And what we are contending for is not just small-scale happiness but large-scale greatness of some kind—maybe money, maybe fame.

Of course, for Shakespeare's characters, the striving lasts longer than Andy Warhol's fifteen minutes, and the stakes are higher and bloodier, and God knows it all gets expressed in a language that is the most awesome use of English there is. But the central energy is still the same. There is the looking forward, the striving to go from rags to riches, or from servitude to crown, or from lover to ass and back to lover again. There's that sense of being part of "a brave new world that has such people in it." That's us. And that's Shakespeare's plays.

## Style is an arrangement of truth

*Style* is the word people in acting circles use for plays and movies that are not contemporary realism. This includes "theatrical" material like Brecht or Beckett plays; dramas with mythological characters, from Greek tragedies to *Harry Potter* movies; material about specific cultures, from lyrical Irish plays to movies like *Witness* or *Braveheart*; and, finally, material from historical periods, including Shakespeare.

When you act in a style piece, there's a temptation to concentrate too much on the "trimmings" they often come with: "cool swords," "fancy clothes," "weird ways of talking," etc. But make an effort, right off the bat, to think less about that stuff and more about the flesh-and-blood character underneath it all. Otherwise you'll end up playing so-called theatrical plays in a way that looks like you're doing acting exercises, or doing a character in an Irish drama who sounds like a leprechaun, or giving performances of kings or queens who look like they're posing for portraits.

Sometimes actors think of style pieces as being "less truthful" than modern drama. We can be condescending in the way we think about people from other places and times; we assume they weren't as "real" as we are today. But characters in style pieces are no less true than we are. The only difference is that their *truth is arranged by their circumstances*.

In our own lives we, too, have times when the circumstances arrange our truth in a way that gives our behavior a *style* we don't usually have. When you walk down the aisle as the member of a wedding party, you don't walk in the same way you do in a mall. It's not a false walk, just a walk that has been slightly rearranged by the solemnity of the situation. That's style.

Histories and societies are, in essence, sets of *rules*, the rules of a given place and time. And it's these rules that create stylistic differences.

An adolescent girl walks down the street in short-shorts and a bathing-suit bra, giggling with her girlfriends. If it's a street in America, it's perfectly normal. But if the street is in one of those countries that stone adulterers, she's in trouble. Same young girl, same giggle—different rules, which demand different styles. But all equally truthful.

So when you do plays of style, think of the character as someone who eats and sleeps and shits and scratches. Then—adding as you go throughout the research and rehearsal process—let your understanding of the "rules" of the character's society and time period shape a true person, not a "character."

I once said to an actor doing Shakespeare, "You look like you're in a Shakespeare play." "But," he argued, "I *am* in a Shakespeare play." To which I replied, "Yes, but *the character* doesn't know that." Maybe that's the best way to test your work in a style piece: ask yourself if you look like you have on *clothes* or *a costume*. If you seem less like it's *your* armor being worn into a battle, and more like you're on your way to a Halloween party, you're doing it wrong. "Style" is something to be *lived*, not just *played*.

I saw Ian McKellen do a modern-dress production of *Richard III*. Many an actor who plays Richard III will emphasize Richard's infamous humpback, acting almost like the character woke up and discovered the hump that morning rather than having been born with it and living with it his whole life. But McKellen did the reverse, to amazing effect.

He left one entire side of his body paralyzed, and using his *one* arm, he got himself dressed, head to toe, in full military uniform: belts, buckles, hat, gloves, the works. And he did it with such ease, as if he had done it every day of his life. Which of course the character had. I'm sure it took hours and hours for the actor to achieve what he did. But worth it.

## *Don't use a false voice*

When you do Shakespeare, don't all of a sudden start lapsing into a faux British accent, like some actors do. It makes no sense at all. While Shakespeare happened to live in England, most of his plays are not set there. It would be more appropriate to play Macbeth with a Scottish accent rather than an English one, since the play is set in Scotland. Or to play Hamlet with a Danish accent (Can you imagine?).

It is better to speak in whatever accent you yourself might have and allow Shakespeare's words to shape your speech into a more fitting sound—which they will, over time. While no one wants to hear Shakespeare done with a thick New York accent or a Fargo twang, the fact is that general American speech (with all its earthiness and texture) is much closer to the sound of Elizabethan speech than contemporary British speech, as any credible linguistic scholar will tell you.

Second, when you speak Shakespeare, don't highlight those stereotypical "Shakespeare words" like *hath, doth, whilst, coudst, woudst, wherefore, quoth*. While they may *seem* to be quintessential "Shakespeare" to us, these words, in his day, were like our simple everyday words such as *had, did, while, could, would, why, say.* We say: "You are an *ass.*" We don't say: "You are *an* ass." So, in Shakespeare, say, "He doth *love.*" Don't say, "He *doth* love." Try to make these inconsequential words seem common; make them throwaways; let them roll off your tongue with ease. You'll be amazed how much more realistic you will sound and how much clearer the meaning of what you are saying will be.

Finally, don't feel obliged to affect one of those "beautiful Shakespearean voices." I actually find those voices a little tiresome after a while. Those famous British Shakespearean baritones sound impressive in commercial voice-overs, but I once saw one of them do *The Merchant of Venice,* and after three hours of plumy tones and perfect elocution I would have been happy to have him replaced in the last act by Jerry Lewis.

I'm more partial to those Shakespearean actors who don't have overdetermined, easily imitated, one-trick sounds. I mean people like Ben Kingsley, Peter O'Toole, Vanessa Redgrave, Kevin Kline, Sam Waterston. Their voices are free and *flexible.* They aren't stuck in one color or tone but are able to contour to the nuance and modulations of the character's feelings. A *real* voice is always better than a so-called beautiful voice. You're playing characters, not announcers.

## Make each word sound like what it means

In an experiment I've done many times with actors who are new to Shakespeare, I divide a roomful of them into two groups and send one of the groups out of the room. I then have someone from the remaining group to get up and read a Shakespearean sonnet. Afterward I ask everyone what the poem they just heard was about. Usually they have only a vague idea: *"It's about spring-time, or something . . . and lips, I think."*

I take aside the actor who read the sonnet and whisper an acting note to him. Then I call the group from outside back into the room and ask the actor to read the sonnet to *them*, this time using what I told him or her to do. Afterward I ask the second group what the sonnet was about. To the amazement of the first group, the people who heard the *second* rendition of the sonnet have a much greater grasp of both the meaning and images of the poem.

The note I give to the actor who reads is very simple. I tell him to make each word *sound like what it means.* For example, if the actor says the word "evil," to make the "v" sound "sinister"; for the word "plead," to draw out the "e," as though the actor is in pain.

When you make the words in Shakespeare sound like what they mean, it does two things. First, it makes for more variety in the music of your speech. But it also makes the *meaning* of what is being said a lot clearer, because very often the meaning and personality of the word are expressed by the sound of the word—the music of it. It's uncanny how many words in English *do* sound like what they mean. You can't say "guts" without sounding like you were just punched in the guts; you can't say "smile" without smiling—and thus sounding like you're smiling, or say "spring" without sounding like a spring. And on and on.

Shakespeare in particular took advantage of this in his writing. *His meaning is often in the music.* And the music comes from his word choice.

If you were able to unlearn English so that you could hear Shakespeare's language as pure sound, pure music, with no awareness of word definitions, you would probably be able to get much of the meaning of what was being said, and all of the emotional *tone* of what was being said, just by the way the sounds of certain words landed on your ear and made you feel.

To show you just how much Shakespeare loved interesting sounding and aptly toned words, take a look at the following list. This amazing variety, this feast of descriptive sounds, are from just *one* act of *one* play (*Romeo and Juliet*, Act I).

As you go through the words, say them aloud. And try to *make each one sound like what it means.* You'll be amazed at what a workout you'll get, and what a juicy and vivid language English can be in the hands of Shakespeare and a good actor.

*dignity, grudge, mutiny, loins, strike, bite, heartless, hate, crutch, profane, pernicious, mistempered, cankered, defiance, hissed, thrusts, affections, fray, brawling, misshapen, sparkling, choking, groan, sick, chastity, assailing, saint-seducing, sparring, reckoning, marred, treading, limping, delight, giddy, desperate, infection, rank, shut, whipped, tormented, beauteous, lovely, lively, crutch, drowned, burnt, crystal, scant, rejoice, earthquake, wormwood, nipple, waddled, wretch, perilous, bitterly, sucked, valiant, precious, beauty, extremity, hoodwinked, enpierced, tender, rough, pricking, deformities, tickle, senseless, whip, stickest, gallop, curtsies, blisters, plagues, cutting, untangled, fantasy, frozen, angered, puffs, despised, vile, lusty, scrape, brisk, unplagued, whispering, scorn, illbeseeming, mutiny, saucy, trick, tremble, bitterest, profane, growl, sprung, loathed, groaned, passion*

## When people really mean something, they pronounce it well

When you say something that you feel strongly, you always pronounce it well. If you say to someone, in a very serious argument, "You're an idiot!" they usually don't say, "Eh? Come again. What did you say—I'm an Indian?" They hear it loud and clear, because you pronounce it completely. And that's the key—*to squeeze every ounce of feeling out of every syllable of every word.*

A good rule of thumb is to think that, when you really mean what you say, *there is no such thing as a single syllable*: every syllable is really three syllables. In the same way that parents will use their child's *full name* when they're angry ("Michael Sean Anderson, get over here!"), a similar thing happens when we say things that matter to us. We use the full "three syllables" of every syllable, so to speak. When we mean it, we say say "hate" as HHH–AAAYYY–TTT, spitting out that "t." We say "great" as GER–ATE–TAH!

But bear in mind that, given the notion that meaning what you say helps you pronounce it well, the reverse must also be true: *if you pronounce something well you will sound like you really mean it*. And that's a good trick for an actor to know.

*Pronounce fully* and you will come across with greater command. People assume the "fuller pronouncer" really means what he says. It's why people think that Brits are so much smarter than Americans. They aren't, they just pronounce better than us, so they *sound* smarter.

One final note of caution. The goal is *not* to pronounce a word "properly" as if you were in an elocution class; the goal is to pronounce the word *fully*. People who hear you shouldn't think, "Oh that actor is trying to overpronounce the words."

In all of these vocal adjustments, try to err on the side of being subtle and not overly actor-y.

## Don't automatically stop at the line breaks

If there were one thing I could change about how Americans are exposed to Shakespeare, it would be the way his published plays are *typeset*. The plays are printed in a format of ten-syllable lines, meaning the written text stops after ten syllables, and the next line down begins with a capital letter, as you would normally find at the beginning of a sentence. For example:

O' for a muse of fire that will ascend
The brightest heaven of invention.

The way the line looks on the page in this format, especially in a long speech, tends to freak out Americans. We see this format and think there must be some fancy reason why the line stops there, so when we either read or speak the speech we tend to *halt* a bit at the end of the line. But when you say it that way—"O' for a muse of fire that will ascend *(stop)* the brightest heaven of invention"—it sounds to the listener like the sentence ends at the stop, which it doesn't. So, then, when you start up with the next part of the line: "The brightest heaven of invention" the listener thinks a new sentence is starting. So when nothing else comes we think, "Yeah . . . so . . . what about 'the brightest heaven of invention'?" And the meaning ends up all botched.

I've always felt the whole thing would be easier if the plays were just typeset so that a line like this would read: *O' for a Muse of fire that will ascend the brightest heaven of invention.* Which would make more sense.

But there are reasons why Shakespeare's plays are set in this traditional format. It was the convention in his day, so the first printed texts of his plays were printed in this format, and that's what has been passed down to us. (The format can actually be quite helpful to people who study Shakespearean verse forms, and to actors who are fairly advanced in their understanding of Shakespearean rhythms. But more about that in a later note.)

If you are fairly new to Shakespeare, the typeset format won't be a problem for you if you train yourself to keep *reading right through to the periods* or semicolons. Ignore the line breaks, ignore the capital letter that begins the next line, and carry your eye and your voice and your understanding of what's being said all the way through to the punctuation mark that indicates a "stop."

On the page it's:

The brightness of her cheek would shame those
    stars,
As daylight doth a lamp; her eyes in heaven
Would through the airy region stream so bright
That birds would sing and think it were not night.

When you read it should be:

The brightness of her cheek would shame those
stars as daylight doth a lamp. Her eyes in heaven
would through the airy region stream so bright that
birds would sing and think it were not night.

You may even want to retype your lines this way, which
can be helpful at first.


## *Keep commas up, put periods to rest*

Punctuation isn't something actors usually pay much attention to, but in dealing with Shakespeare and other
historical or "language" plays it can be your best friend.
So *use it*.

In Shakespeare, punctuation is like a closet organizer. It organizes the meaning of what's being said by
keeping together what should be together, and preventing what shouldn't be together from getting mixed up.
There's a very funny scene in *A Midsummer Night's
Dream* about what happens when the organization of
punctuation goes haywire, when a nervous amateur
actor does a prologue before royalty in which his

catawampus punctuating makes lines like "*Our true intent is all for your delight! We are not here that you should here repent you*" come out of his panicked mouth to the appalled listeners as:

> *Our true intent is. All for your delight we are not here!*
> *That you should here repent! You!*

Shakespeare was a man who knew that, on stage, *the actor is the embodiment of punctuation* and therefore an organizer of meaning for the audience.

But beyond meaning, there is also the music of speech. As you get better at using it, punctuation can be like musical notations in sheet music. It gives you ideas about how the rhythm and emotional "pitch" of a speech should be handled—almost as if punctuation is the conductor, with you as the orchestra.

Here are some tips for using specific punctuation marks. First, the comma—the most frequently used punctuation mark in Shakespeare. Because there are so many commas in his texts, if you pause at each one his speeches will seem endless and you'll never get any excitement or momentum going.

They're called commas, not *comas*. So don't pause at every one.

In fact, think the reverse: a comma is not a cue to stop but a push to keep the speech going forward. When you come to a comma, let the tone of your voice tell us there's *more to come* rather than making it sound like something is ending. Take these lines of Lady Macbeth's, for example.

Come, thick night,
And pall thee in the dunnest smoke of hell,
That my keen knife see not the wounds it makes,
Nor heaven peep through the blanket of the dark,
To cry, "Hold, Hold!"

Rather than go: "Come *[stop]* thick night *[stop]* and pall thee in the dunnest smoke of hell *[stop]* that my keen knife . . ." etc. Think instead of the comma as an arrow [ > ] that points us forward and pushes us on, as if it were saying, "Hey audience, something important is coming up next! Stay awake, Pay attention. Here it comes." As in: "Come > thick night > and pall thee in the dunnest smoke of hell > that my keen knife sees not the wounds it makes > nor heaven peep through the blanket of the dark to cry > 'Hold! Hold!'"

Try speaking any Shakespearean speech by making small stops at the commas. Then speak it again, keeping the commas "up." You'll be amazed at the difference, how fast it goes and how much momentum is generated by "upwardly" inflecting your commas.

It's a lesson that was driven home to me years ago by a wonderfully eccentric old British voice teacher I had. (How could you not like a voice teacher who chain-smoked Dunhills and put gin in her coffee?) Whenever actors in her speech class let their commas "droop," as she described it, she would holler things like, *"Keep your peckers up!"* or *"Haven't you ever noticed that a comma looks just like a limp willy?!"* (As acting notes go, these were memorable ones.)

If you have used your commas to maintain the forward progress and upward momentum of a speech, you want to use the period as a way of coming to a dramatic *stop*. When you come to the period, give the line a "sense of an ending," to lend the verse a quality of winding down into a rest from all the motion that has been generated by keeping your commas up. In order to do this, think that, at a period, you are putting what you say *to rest*. Really let the moment *land* before sending the speech back into flight.

Look at this speech of Miranda's from *The Tempest* in which she pleads with her magician father to help a ship in peril. If you keep the comma "up" but don't kill the periods, it can come cross as a shrill harangue, with one idea bleeding into the next:

> If by your art, my dearest father, you have
> Put the wild waters in this roar, allay them.
> The sky it seems would pour down stinking pitch,
> But that the sea, mounting to the welkin's cheek,
> Dashes the fire out. O! I have suffer'd . . .

But if you "kill" the periods you begin to create more emotional nuance. And this putting to rest always works with Shakespeare because he tends to put the "idea" that he's talking about to rest right at the end of a sentence, just before the period. In this speech, "allay them" comes just before the period—and the word actually *means* "to put to rest." Then, just before the other period, she says, "dashes the fire out"—again, a putting to rest of something.

Try Miranda's speech both ways: once where you keep the whole thing up, once where you really put the *periods* to rest. You'll hear how much better it is the second way. Face it: many "style" pieces tend to be wordy. But this little technique can help you fill long speeches with all the exciting "rises and falls" of the dramatic roller-coaster rides they were written to be.

## If a word's meaning is difficult, play its feel

When you ask American audiences the greatest obstacle to understanding Shakespeare, they'll usually say, "The language is too difficult."

But the language is English!

Of course you will sometimes come to a passage that *seems* like another language, but not often. More likely you will come to a single word or phrase that you don't understand. So what! The same could be said for many shows on TV that you might be asked to do as an actor. There are all kinds of specialized, technical vocabulary on cop shows or lawyer shows, but no actor will say, "I can't audition for *CSI* because the language is too difficult." When you do those shows, you find out what the strange words mean (e.g., "gamma globulin" or "lumenal"), then you do your best to get that meaning across to your audience. Same thing with Shakespeare.

In most editions of Shakespeare there is a helpful glossary of words and phrases, often right on the page itself, that will explain the meaning to you. Look up the word and then try to put it in a sentence that you would actually speak. I know it sounds like a grammar-school exercise, but it helps make the words your own. And that will come in handy when you face the challenge of "explaining" those meanings to an audience by the way you act them.

When you come to a word that a modern audience probably won't understand, you must work doubly hard to play the *tone, personality, and mood* of the word or phrase.

For example, in *The Merchant of Venice* there is a line in which Shylock says to Antonio, "You that did void your rheum upon my beard." Clearly "void your rheum" is not a phrase *we* use every day, so it won't be readily apparent to a modern audience. But the word "void" in this sense means *spit*, and the word "rheum" means *phlegm* or *mucus*. All the actor needs to do is play the tone, personality, and mood of what Shylock is saying and, given the revolting images, that shouldn't be hard for an actor to do.

A cautionary note: avoid doing cheap mimelike or charadelike gestures to get across meaning. Were an actor who had the Shylock line to make a noise like coughing up phlegm while saying it, I would think him a cheap actor to say the least.

(I once saw an actor mime shooting an arrow while saying Hamlet's "slings and arrows." *Never try to make up in mime what you lack in acting ability.* There should be a special place in hell for actors who crotch-grab, crotch-thrust, or mime feeling themselves up—the universal bad-actor sign for "boobs.")

## Think of the verse pattern as a pulse

Most people with a little experience in Shakespeare have at least heard the term *iambic pentameter,* the form of verse in which Shakespeare most often wrote.

Here's the nutshell version. In iambic pentameter, each line of verse is ten syllables long, with the *accent* coming on every other syllable, as in: "Now *is* the *win*ter *of* our *discontent*." Simply put, it has a kind of dee-*dum* dee-*dum* dee-*dum* rhythm.

While the term iambic pentameter may sound like something that would appear on a grammar midterm, it is just a fancy phrase for something that is very natural, very human. This dee-*dum*-dee-*dum*-dee-*dum* rhythm underlies the most basic things in life: heartbeat, respiration, footsteps, sex.

Iambic pentameter is the rhythm of life, the music of being human.

It's not about keeping an overdone dee-*dum* beat. Always think *tension* more than *beat*. When you hit the constant dee-*dum*-dee-*dum* too hard it can make the verse sound like a nursery rhyme, and Shakespeare is not Mother Goose. Iambic pentameter isn't the drums in the band; it's the bass. The heartbeat. Think of the rhythm as if it were an actual *pulse*—like the way your blood pulsates through your veins when the heart pounds because of emotion. Iambic pentameter isn't bongo drums; it's the throbbing blood pressure caused by feeling. The beats don't get *faster,* they get *stronger.* Like a pounding heart.

When you speak Shakespeare, try to sustain the tension of the rhythm. Imagine there's a taut string holding together beads of words. If you let the string go slack, his lines tend to sound too sloppy or loose or choppy. It also slows down the speech and makes the whole thing feel like you're driving with the emergency brake on.

But when you sustain that rhythm it keeps the music of the speech tight, and nicely tense. You start to feel like you're riding the words and they're doing the work for you. John Gielgud said:

> I think many young actors fail to understand what Shakespeare's language has to offer them. Good verse-speaking is rather like swimming. If you surrender to the water it keeps you up, but if you fight you drown.

The wave is already there for you, all you have to do is get on it and go. And *that*, to me, is iambic pentameter.

Finally, you'll notice that at times Shakespeare changes this ten-syllable dee-*dum* rhythm. When that happens, it's almost like a heart that either skips a beat or quickens because of what the person may be feeling: fear, anger, love. His most famous line breaks the iambic pentameter pattern: *"To be or not to be, that is the question."* Count it; it's *eleven* syllables, almost as if Hamlet's unresolved mind makes his heart flutter an *extra* beat at the end of the line.

Remember: all language started as music, and the great poets bring it back to that.

## Do a list as either a ladder or a storyboard

Shakespeare made terrific lists. Time and again he will give a character a verbal riff in which they tick off, in a listlike progression, a series of images. Here's one from his most famous speech, in which Hamlet "lists" seven reasons for despair:

> For who would bear *the whips and scorns of time*,
> The *oppressor's wrong*, the *proud man's contumely*,

The *pangs of despis'd love*, the *law's delay*,
The *insolence of office*, and the *spurns*
*That patient merit of the unworthy takes* . . .

When confronted with this in Shakespeare, handle it in one of two ways. First, think of the list as a *ladder*. This means you make each image from the list *add* to your emotional intensity—you *build* to something, with each item on the list kicking you up a notch. In this speech Hamlet is clearly showing how many things are "rotten in the state of Denmark," so a ladder would show his mounting despair.

The other way to handle a Shakespearean list is to make it a *storyboard*. When you storyboard you take each image in the list and *etch* it; you create a specific picture unto itself. When you storyboard, you put less focus on the rising momentum of the list, as you would in a ladder, and instead you work to show the detail of each of the phrases or pictures. You consciously try to make each one distinct from the others.

In Shakespeare, much of the energy of speaking comes from the effort a character puts into getting his or her point across clearly. When you work to make what you're saying *ascend* in a ladder, or work to forge ideas into the specific, pounded-out *pictures* of a storyboard, the aerobics of that effort can make language exciting to speak and thrilling to hear.

## Notice and use the simple, one-syllable words

There is no getting around the fact that America has always had a distrust of words. Especially big words, fancy words, words that are known only by the "educated elite" and not the masses.

A good vocabulary is resented by some Americans as being almost "undemocratic."

Americans prefer plainer talk. When it comes to politics, we usually elect the candidate we find to be the more "plainspoken" of the two. When it comes to movies, the evil heavy in the action film is the one who is a fancy talker (usually an alumnus from the Royal Shakespeare Company who's come over to bag some Hollywood money). The heavy has the elegant voice and a big, fancy vocabulary while our American hero has a gritty voice and never uses any word that might (heaven forbid) go over the head of anyone sitting in NASCAR bleachers.

Without question, many "style" or "period" plays are wordy. And Shakespeare's plays are feasts of words. But rather than being frustrated by this barrage of words, look at it this way: words were to entertainment in Shakespeare's day what *images* are to entertainment in *our* day. In the same way that we put dozens of images in montage form in the space of one thirty-second commercial, in the pre-media days, people had only *words* and not *pixels* to show off with, and show off they did. In the same way we like to put in twenty quick images when one would do, they liked saying with a dozen words what could have been said with a few. So, just as you may complain that Shakespeare's work is too wordy, perhaps five hundred years from now students will look back at our culture, turn up their noses, and say, "It was too image-y."

*The trick is to try to find in Shakespeare those moments of language that don't intimidate you but touch you.*

And they are plentiful. Although his language is heightened, it's amazing how often Shakespeare uses the smallest and simplest words when he is expressing something the character feels deeply. Winston Churchill once said, "The best words are small words; and the best words of all are small, old words." Shakespeare will *often* use small, old words at some of his character's most heartfelt moments.

The most famous line of all, "To be or not to be, that is the question," is all single syllable words except one. Small and old and simple. And he does this in play after play. Romeo says, "O it is my love. O that she knew she were." Lear says, "Fool, I shall go mad." Iago says, "I am not what I am." Lady Macbeth says, "Out, out damned spot." Richard II says, "I live with bread like you, feel want, taste grief, need friends."

And this next one is the most moving one of all, to me. It was written around the time that Shakespeare's real son Hamnet died at age eleven. It is a speech from the play *King John* in which the character of Constance refers to her dead child as

*"My life, my joy, my food, my all the world."*

All simple, short, old words; all monosyllabic—but, what writing! To call someone "my *food*" because you love them so much—what a perfect, visceral way of describing it.

And then the phrase I can never get out of my head: *"my all the world."*

I have often wondered if this was something Shakespeare actually said to his little boy who died, or maybe wrote to him. I can almost picture it written on a ribbon that hangs off a spray of flowers on a child's casket. "My all the world." So simple. So Shakespeare.

Always look for these monosyllabic and *spare* lines. Give them the kind of unadorned directness and lack of fuss that good American acting always has. It should be as if the play stops, Shakespeare stops, great language stops, acting stops, and all you are left with is a human being communicating simply.

---

## Summary of Notes on Shakespeare

1. *Don't be intimidated because you are American.*
2. *Style is an arrangement of truth.*
3. *Don't use a false voice.*
4. *Make each word sound like what it means.*
5. *When people really mean something, they pronounce it well.*
6. *Don't automatically stop at the line breaks.*
7. *Keep commas up, put periods to rest.*
8. *If a word's meaning is difficult, play its feel.*
9. *Think of the verse pattern as a pulse.*
10. *Do a list as either a ladder or a storyboard.*
11. *Notice and use the simple, one-syllable words.*

---

# CHAPTER EIGHT

# STAGE
# AND SCREEN

*The difference is dimensional*

Years ago I saw the Broadway production of the play *Bent*. It starred a then up-and-coming film star, Richard Gere, and a well-established theater actor named David Dukes. I thought Gere was a little dull compared to Dukes, who seemed to blow Gere off the stage. I left that show thinking that Dukes was far and away a better actor.

I later saw Dukes on several TV shows and in a couple of movies and was amazed at how much less I liked his acting *on screen*. He came across as mannered, a little hammy, and just not very believable. I was forced to rethink my feelings about him. Just as I was forced to rethink my feelings about Gere when I saw him, over the years, give some excellent screen performances.

I realized there is a big difference between acting on stage and acting on screen, and some actors are just more naturally suited to one or the other. I also realized that any actor who wants to be good at both has to be able to *make adjustments* in his or her acting to suit each medium. This begins with an understanding of the difference in their "dimensions."

The theater is a *three-dimensional* experience. The audience looks at you as if you were a moving sculpture. They see how your body and your personal energy interact with the space around you. And the audience is, of course, at a distance from you, so they tend to like an actor who seems—in personality and physicality—to "come to them." That's why it's the Zero Mostels, the Zoe Caldwells, the Colleen Dewhursts, and the Nathan Lanes who are the theater greats. As an audience, you feel like they "come to you."

Film, on the other hand, is two-dimensional. In film the audience looks at you as if you were a painting, and they *need to sense that you are at ease existing within the limits of that flat dimension.* If the film actor's acting ever seems like it's starting to "come out at the audience," the audience subliminally senses you pushing the envelope of the two-dimensional, and it breaks the spell of the fantasy—not overtly, but enough to feel something in your acting they are not comfortable watching on screen.

Great film actors, from Garbo to Robert Redford to Julia Roberts to George Clooney, seem to ignore even the possibility of the "third-dimension" because they are so comfortable living within the two-dimensional plane of the screen. Consequently, audiences are comfortable losing themselves in the movie's world through the actor's easy performance.

Now, what can actors do—what little mental trick can they apply—to feel the difference of the two planes?

Try this exercise. Take a bit of a monologue, maybe a page or so in length. Something simple and realistic. Do it first "three-dimensionally." Imagine that you are *inside the monologue,* meaning that you put whatever is occurring in the speech—everything that it talks about or deals with—*around you,* as though it were happening with you *in its midst.* If you choose "To be or not to be," put the "slings and arrows" and that "outrageous fortune" around you; put yourself *inside the action* of it.

Now try it two-dimensionally. Put the monologue *inside of you.* Imagine that whatever is occurring in the monologue is happening *in* you, not around you. Again, if it's slings, arrows, and fortune, gather them up in your mind and inside your body. Think of something that the director George Stevens once said: "Film acting is talking soft and thinking loud."

Trying the same monologue these two different ways will give you a feel of the "dimensional difference" between film and theater acting.

## The difference isn't in how you do things but in what you choose to do

One actor who, in my opinion, was equally good on stage *and* screen was Jason Robards. He was one of the best all-around actors ever, as his back-to-back Oscars for films and record-breaking Tony nominations for theater attest.

No matter which medium he acted in, Robards was believable, emotionally complex, and commanding in his performances. When he acted on stage, Robards could be heard and felt in the farthest row of the theater, but when he was on film he made you feel like you were eavesdropping on a real person, looking at him through a keyhole. (Rent the movie *Julia* or *All the President's Men* to see what I mean.)

It was amazing to watch him go back and forth between mediums with equal excellence. Like a magician, he made you scratch your head and ask, "How'd he do it?" But also like a magician, I think he had a trick.

The difference between what Robards did on stage and what he did on film was not so much *the way* he did things but *what he chose to do.*

What he did on stage was never done in a big and showy *way*; and what he did on film was never done in a tiny and cautious *way*. He never adjusted the truth of what his character was supposed to be feeling to fit the scale of the different mediums. There was always baseline honesty in "the way" he did *everything.*

The difference was in *what he chose to do* to express the character. He chose behaviors that he knew were true to the character but also fit the specifications of whatever medium he was working in. On film he would *glance* with only his eyes, whereas on stage he might *turn* his head. On film he would *furrow* his brow to express his character's vulnerability, whereas on stage he might *shrug* his shoulders. On film he would *close his eyes* in sadness; on stage he would *sit down* sadly in a chair.

He made equally apt vocal choices. On film he spoke no louder than was needed to have a microphone pick up his words, but he made this way of speaking natural to his character. His style of speech expressed editor Ben Bradlee's workaday way of tossing off orders to subordinates in *All the President's Men*, just as the gravelly subtlety of his way of talking in *Julia* expressed the morose confidence of his character Dashiell Hammett.

On stage he seemed to take an entirely different vocal approach. His booming voice amply filled the theater, all the way up to the balcony where I sat when I saw him in a revival of Eugene O'Neill's *The Iceman Cometh*. But he didn't just project his *voice*, he projected his *character*. Rather than force a falsely loud voice onto his role, he used the full volume to express the traits of his character—like Hickey's need to show off and his salesman's self-confidence. As a result, the loud voice seemed like the most natural thing in the world for this character—Hickey's normal means of self-expression.

Robard's trick of making smart choices gave him the right level of expressiveness for the medium and the best approach to simple, truthful behavior.

*In real life our level of expressiveness constantly changes because of the situation, without affecting the basic truth of our feeling changing.*

Person No. 1 sits alone at a desk in front of a computer, to compose the eulogy of a friend. Someone he loved. As he writes, the person feels everything he puts down on paper. Person No. 2 gets up in front of a roomful of people and reads the eulogy of a friend they all loved. Both people have the same level of feeling and the same level of truth; they are merely in situations that ask for a different level of expressiveness.

Simply put: film acting is writing the eulogy; stage acting is delivering the eulogy.

## *In theater, stillness works like a close-up does on screen*

Next time you see one of those "behind the scenes" TV shows about the making of a movie, notice what the director spends his or her time doing on the set. They aren't talking to actors about their performances, that's for sure. Their sole focus seems to be on things like framing, lenses, and camera movements as they give their full attention to the technical demands of *getting the shot.*

But audiences go to films to see actors, not lenses. Right? So why is camera work such a priority to film directors? Because they know they have the power to *control the attention* of the audience by what they give them to look at.

Theater actors would do well to learn from this notion. Too often an actor will go on stage *assuming* the audience will pay attention to him. But that's not the case. There are a lot of other interesting things on that wide and brightly lit stage that an audience can look at besides you.

*A stage actor cannot "assume" the audience's attention. He or she has to "take" it.*

Believe it or not, the best way to get an audience's attention in the theater is by using a strong, controlled *stillness.*

Try this experiment with another actor. Take a few steps toward the actor and say (seriously) the line,

"They want to talk to you." Repeat the line, using the same inflection and level of intensity. The first time you deliver the line, do it while you are *still moving* toward the person. The second time, *stop walking, be still*, then speak the line.

Ask your partner which version was more effective and I guarantee the actor will say the *second* one, even though he or she may not be able to say exactly why. The reason is that the human eye reacts more quickly than the human ear. Furthermore, the eye reacts involuntarily whereas the ear can tune things out. *On stage, stillness functions like a film close-up: it makes the audience focus on you.*

When an actor is moving on stage, the audience's attention is naturally drawn toward that movement. But when the actor grows still, the eyes of the audience are deprived of that movement. So they look up to your face and transfer their attention to what you are saying—just like a camera lens pushing in for a close-up.

One of the things that separates a good stage actor from a bad one is that a good actor can maintain a strong stillness while the bad stage actor fidgets. Theater actors should cultivate their ability to be still. It gets attention.

## In theater, your performance needs to be shaped

Beauty is a matter of shape. From the shaped marble of a sculpture to the shaped sound of a musical score to the shapely contours of the physically attractive body, shape determines beauty. Humans have a primal capacity to identify something as beautiful by filtering it through their individual ideals of shape.

When it comes to acting, your goal should be to contour the emotional energy of your characterization into a performance that has an actual *sense of shape* to it.

Actors often give earnest attention to issues like character psychology, interpretation, blocking, and lines, but they barely consider the *shape* of their performance. Yet audiences do perceive the "shape" of your acting. They feel how an actor makes his energy rise, recede, build, and burst. They can even feel when your performance is shapeless.

In film the director and particularly the film editor do this "shaping" *for* the actor. The biggest determining factor in why a film does or does not "click" is the finished shape in which the film emerges from the editing room. That's why the most powerful person on the production is the one who gets the so-called "final cut."

When it comes to theater, the actor always has the final cut. And many stage performances could benefit from "editing" to give them better shape.

*The greatest tool that stage actors have to shape their performance is the way they pace their dialogue.* A play is pulled along by *its lines. They* control the pace of the performance. Theater has always been less visual than film and more "auditory." (During the Renaissance, people would say they were "going to *hear* a play," not *see* it.)

*The key to pacing is the removal of dead air between lines.*

Note that pacing is not about speeding your line. That's a common misconception. Rather, it is more about cutting out the "gaps" between the end of another actor's lines and the beginning of your line, in the same way that an editor will lop off a frame or two of film to make for crisper pacing.

At times you should almost overlap your partner's dialogue, coming in right at the ends of his or her lines. In some cases it can be more effective to overlap them outright (with the partner's permission, of course). Then, when there *is* a full stop in the conversation, it matters. Like a rest note in a musical score, that stop is *part of the music*, not a halt in the music. Silences can be a great shaping tool. Don't waste them.

"Editing your dialogue" like this will also make you sound a lot more realistic, because that's how people talk in real life. Next time you are out in public, within earshot of strangers having a conversation, eavesdrop. You'll notice there is hardly any *gap* when one person finishes talking and the other starts. (Thus that famous expression about having trouble "getting a word in edgewise.")

Try it, it works. And it can tighten your performance.

## *In theater, go beyond the text*

Most actors have old scripts lying around everywhere, pages of them crushed into strange origami at the bottom of backpacks, or crammed under the seats of cars. All of them full of penciled-in notes that, when read years later, can make you embarrassed or nostalgic. Actors love their scripts. And who can blame them? They are the only thing an actor has to hold on to (literally) when working on a role. The actor and his script are a *relationship*.

But while the intimacy of actors with their scripts is something all actors know about, you hear very little discussion about how different that actor/script relationship is when you are working on a play as opposed to a film.

Given the way plays are rehearsed, it's normal that everyone in the company should know the entire script. From the first reading on, all the actors—big part or small—hear the script from beginning to end, time and time again. In short order they *all* get used to it, from its specific words and lines to its overall structure.

But this process of "getting used" to a script, which happens so naturally in the theater, can also be damaging. The script can lose its fictional magic and turn into the mere blueprint of a performance, a series of tasks (lines, cues, actions, moments) that must be executed during the course of the play. At which point the script stops being alive and deadens into something rote and unconsidered, something almost cynical.

I once sat in on rehearsals for a production of *A Streetcar Named Desire*. I was struck by the way that everyone in the company—actors, director, stagehands—referred to Act III, scene 4, as "The Rape Scene." It was said over and over in such a casual, almost irreverent way that it lost its meaning and became almost funny. Lighting guys hanging from ladders said things like, "Hey, is this the Venetian-blind-pattern gobo that we use for the rape scene?" I actually heard an actor say to his dresser, "No—I use the gray socks for the rape scene."

*That's the occupational hazard of theater acting: the deepest human emotions and issues can become commonplace.*

The only way to prevent this from happening is to keep *reading into* the play. By this I mean you need to keep "reinspiring" the play for yourself and—just as that term implies—keep "breathing" new life into it. Read about the author of the play, read books about the play, or books about the subject matter the play deals with. Listen to music that you think may relate to the story, or music that just inspires you. Look around in your everyday life for any bit of stimulus that you can bring back to the play. I once knew an actor playing a part in a Dickens piece who would stop at a local dog pound to look at those sad-eyed orphans whenever he felt the script had stopped touching him.

Over a long run, the play is simply not enough for an actor. Its fire needs constant kindling.

## In theater, the great actor changes the room

I so believe that the essence of great acting is (a phrase I use a lot) "changing the room," that for a time I toyed briefly with making it the title of this book.

The legendary acting teacher Stella Adler was one of the grand divas of the American theater. She once entered a party at which a little girl was attending with her mother. The child took one look at Adler, turned to her mother, and said, "Mommy, is that god?"

Now that's "changing the room."

Of course, not every stage actor will have as much "presence" as Stella Adler, but all good ones have *some* presence. The law of theater acting is: *You are boring until proven fascinating.* So when you act in theater you need to bring to the stage something that sparks it up.

The great stage actors can turn what Stanislavski called "the creative state" into a very tangible kind of electricity. When a good stage actor enters, the electrical current in the air of the room actually changes. Everyone who's there can feel it happen. It starts even before the actor says a word. As a famous composer once said to the great Broadway musical star Barbara Cook, "You sang eight bars before you even opened your mouth!"

This electricity I'm talking about is no metaphor; it's as real as the energy that lights a lamp. The actress Ellen Burstyn once said, "You can *feel it* go through you." It's palpable.

In the original production of Tennessee Williams's *The Glass Menagerie*, Laurette Taylor gave what Broadway historians call "the single greatest performance in the history of the American theater." While no film footage exists of this performance, every major actor who saw it called it the greatest acting they had ever witnessed. And actor after actor went back to see it multiple times. (Uta Hagen, no slouch herself, saw it *thirteen* times.) It was, by all accounts, as near to magic as acting gets.

When Spencer Tracy—not exactly a guy who needed acting lessons—went backstage after seeing Taylor's performance, he begged, "Help me, Laurette! How do you do it?" According to an eyewitness to the meeting, here's what happened:

She reached down, picked up one of her feet and lifted it so that we could see its blistered and bleeding sole. She dropped it and showed us her other sole. The same.

"That's how," she said. "I grab that goddam stage with my two feet and send it right up from there through the rest of me and out to them."

She makes it sound as if there were some electromagnetic force that fixed her to the floor of the stage and sent a current right through her.

While all of this may sound a bit weird, we do use a lot of electrical imagery to describe great theater performances: *He lit up the stage! She shines! Sparkle! Brilliant! Dazzle! Luminous! Magnetic! Radiant!*

To break this down to an acting note: What if you weren't born with the stage presence of a Stella Adler? What if you've never felt any of this electrical stuff I describe? What are you supposed to do? Go on stage with jumper cables? No. But keep in mind three things.

First: Remember, just because *you* may not have amazing stage presence doesn't mean that *your character* can't have it. We have all seen actors whose performances lit up a theater, only to meet them backstage and find they have no personal spark whatsoever. The shyest, most unassuming actor can find a way to tap into an electrifying characterization.

Second: The only thing that transforms a room faster than "electricity" is *tension*. Tension between people. Have you ever been in a crowded room and watched an argument between two people escalate to a level where the room suddenly turns to hear-a-pin-drop quiet? That's the kind of electricity that any good actor can access and use to change the room of a theater, simply by really connecting with that other actor.

Third: As nutty as this may sound, use the stage lights. A very wise person I know once told me that if an actor concentrates on *allowing his body to absorb the actual theater lights* it can give you a surprising jolt of power. No theater actor to whom I have given this note has failed to be amazed at how well it works.

## *In film, try to avoid the "mask acting" of theater*

Most really good film actors got their start in theater, from Meryl Streep to Sean Penn to Gene Hackman to Annette Bening. Theater is the most common training ground for actors, and still the best. But it is also a medium that can give an actor tendencies and habits that may undermine his or her ability to work in film.

Theater actors tend to use their voices and their bodies in a way that makes a kind of *mask* of their whole acting mechanism. Their voices put a façade of manipulated sound over their words, and they use their bodies to make a façade of emotions: external representations built on hollow gestures and poses of feeling.

This kind of "mask acting," as I call it, can be downright glaring in actors who do a lot of musicals. Haven't you ever seen a musical chorus member come out and say a line like, "The showboat's comin'!" with such a loud, musicalized voice, such hyped-up energy, and such a frozen smile on his face that he does not resemble anything like an actual human being?

If these tendencies become too entrenched in an actor's overall approach to acting, that actor will have a lot of trouble working in film. So an actor should beware of the dangers of "mask acting" early on in his development.

The approach often solidifies during an actor's training years, especially in university theater departments. Because of the kinds of plays that universities like to do (namely, the classics), college theater directors are always looking for actors who can "play age." Because, let's face it, not a lot of the plays in the theater canon are about college-aged characters. (For every Juliet role there are *ten* Lady Capulet roles; for every Alan Strang in *Equus* there are a dozen Martin Dysarts that need to be cast.)

Consequently the people who become the "stars" of the college theater department are the actors who can "play older." (I am talking about the tall, twenty-one-year-old guy with the deep voice and the receding hairline and the large, matronly-looking girl with the husky voice.)

The problem is, when these actors graduate and begin auditioning for films, they are expected to play their *own age.* Actors who have been in play after play in college and have a high (and often well-deserved) opinion of their acting ability get a very rude awakening when they begin making the rounds in the film and TV world. They find out that they never really *learned how to play themselves,* or at least a character who is in *their* demographic, personality type, or age range.

Like it or not, casting directors much prefer actors who simply *are* the character rather than actors who have to *play* it. No matter how "versatile" an actor you are, people in film and TV do not need you to do an uncanny rendition of an elderly, peg-leg Russian guy with a lisp. They will be able to find a *real* elderly, peg-leg Russian actor with a lisp who has an agent and a list of TV credits a mile long.

Actors who hit this wall after a great college "career" are devastated by the disparity between the way they were valued in college and the dismissals they get from film and TV casting people. But the problem is that their college training betrayed them. They emerged from four years of hard work and study with a long list of theater credits but a woefully underdeveloped *sense of self* in their acting.

It's fine to play all those extreme characters in theater, but don't burden your character with an exterior that *masks* the "real you" from the world, or that hides your true self from yourself. In college, *minimize the makeup you use*—like that god-awful gray hair-dye spray that doesn't make a young actor look like an old man but just like a young guy with silver schmutz in his hair.

The technical adjustment you must make to be seen and heard in the theater should always be done to *reveal*, not to *conceal*. Don't use a character to hide the real you, because that's what people who cast films will want to see, so there had better be a *there* there when they get around to looking.

## *In film, the acting isn't smaller, it's closer*

There's a temptation to think that screen acting means that you, as an actor, need to be "smaller" in your acting. But thinking of film acting as being *small* can make your acting too casual and, eventually, *boring*. I find this happens a lot with actors who are in long-running TV shows. Many of them get the "big job" on the show because of some previous work that was thrilling enough to get them noticed. But then, after years on the show, something in their acting diminishes. Their acting grows *small*—first in scale, then, over time, in spirit.

Instead of thinking of film acting as "smaller," think of it as *closer.* While that may seem like a semantic quibble, I think that the word "closer" has connotations that will be more apt to deepen you rather than "shrink" you, while still allowing for a certain naturalness on screen. "Closer" has implications of the personal, the dangerous, the intimate—all good things for actors to strive for.

Keep in mind that *closeness* is the perspective that a film audience has. It's not that they perceive you to be "small"—after all, actors in movies are seen on massive screens. It's that an audience subliminally feels they have an access to you. They look at you from a perspective that puts them nearer to you than to people in their own everyday life. The job of a screen actor is to let people come physically close to you, have access to you, draw so near to you that they are right in your face—without you seeming to be defensive about it.

To help you get better at this, try the following: Perform a scene with a partner, but ask someone else to watch and to function like a camera. The observer shouldn't watch you from out in the audience but should instead stand as close to you as a camera would be. Like a camera, the observer should follow you throughout the scene. At first this will feel weird: half funny, half nerve-racking. But that's what it will be like when you are on a set with a camera filming you, so you need to prepare for it.

Another trick is to try rehearsing a big emotional scene with someone in a small, enclosed space like a closet or an elevator. Again, you may feel nutty doing it, but it will make you a better film actor.

## In film, emotion shouldn't be ugly

In my opinion, the best piece of advice on screen acting is more than four hundred years old and came, of course, from Shakespeare. In Hamlet's "advice to the players," he tells actors what they should and should not do when they play strong emotion. "In the very torrent, tempest and whirlwind of your passion," he says, "you must acquire and beget a temperance that may give it smoothness."

*Smoothness* is the word.

Chances are, when you first saw yourself act on screen you were (1) appalled and (2) felt a desire to tamp down the disjointedness of your facial movements. You wanted to tame it all and, yes, "smooth" out the whole performance so you would look more graceful and watchable, less awkward and frenzied.

It's not uncommon for an actor who is inexperienced at film to feel that he or she did a scene brilliantly, powerfully—only to be horrified when seeing it later on screen. This is especially true if the scene is a highly emotional one. The rush of strong emotion that feels so full and good when you're on a stage in front of an audience can look outsized and, to put it bluntly, grotesque when magnified by the optics of film.

In acting circles there is such a large premium placed on emotion that acting teachers ignore the way emotion can contort an actor's face and make it ugly. But in film this must be taken into account.

Richard Schickel's recent biography of Elia Kazan contains an exchange that is both amusing and very revealing about how emotion transfers to film. It's a discussion between the producer Louis B. Mayer and Kazan of the anatomical details of Katharine Hepburn's on-screen crying:

> Mayer: She cries too much.
> Kazan: But that is the scene, Mr. Mayer.
> Mayer: But the channel of her tears is wrong.
> Kazan: What do you mean?
> Mayer: The channel of her tears goes too close to her nostrils, it looks like it's coming out of her nose like snot.
> Kazan: Jesus, I can't do anything with the channel of her tears.
> Mayer: Young man, you have one thing to learn! We are in the business of making beautiful pictures of beautiful people, and anybody who does not acknowledge that should not be in this business.

The point is, emotion is not enough on film, you also have to be watchable.

One way to help yourself is by working to rid yourself of the extra facial tension that comes when you manufacture emotion. This was something that the great Method guru Lee Strasberg spent a lot of time working on with actors, especially those who were doing a lot of film work at the time. One of his famous students basically defined Strasberg's method this way:

> Economy of style was the rule. We learned we don't belong to the A.F.M.A., Associated Face Makers of America. We learned to say, "I'm very upset" without jutting the jaw out or baring the teeth. We can do chagrin or disappointment or "Holy Shit!" without screwing a face up. We do it every day.

That's realistic acting in a nutshell: you don't belong to the A.F.M.A., you don't do too many annoying things with your face. You feel—but you don't let your passion compromise the picture. Movies are pictures.

## In film, stay within the script

Because of the way movies are made, it's not uncommon for two people with big parts in the same film to meet for the first time at the premiere. Films are shot in small, one-to-two-page chunks, and done so at different locations and out of sequence from the way things happen to your character. All these scattered elements of a film won't be put together into a complete entity until long after your work as an actor is done.

Consequently the written script is the only means you'll have of keeping the structure of the story and the linear development of your character in your head.

Since you'll be filming scenes in a 3, 1, 5, 4, 2 order, it will be useful to remind yourself what those scenes feel like in the 1-to-5 structure as they occur in the script. That's why it's a good idea to read the script *from beginning to end*, again and again.

Being good at plot means you are good at *plotting*— plotting the way your character develops in the scenes. It means you take into consideration the way the audience will receive each scene when they later watch it in sequential order.

I learned a lot by watching screen legend Kirk Douglas rehearse a movie. Every character choice he made was tied to plot. While some actors would ask questions like *What does my character want?* or *What is my character's obstacle?*, Douglas asked questions like *What will the audience have just watched my character do in the scene before this?* or *Do I want to do so much in scene 15, or should I save some of the intensity for scene 31 which should be the climax of the story?* or *Will this be clear enough for the audience to understand why I do what I do in the next scene?*

Douglas was no less wise about character psychology than any die-hard Method actor. He just added to that a wisdom about *audience psychology*. And he did this by keeping the overall design of the story as written in the script uppermost in his mind. It's a knack the film greats seem to have.

## In film, you have to be coordinated

Don't underestimate the onslaught of orders you'll get when acting on a film set. The cameraman will tell you "not to lean back too far in the chair because you'll go out of frame." The script lady will tell you that "You keep saying *his* x-rays, when the actual line is *the* x-rays." The director will tell you things like "Look up-not-down on the first part of the speech, but look down-not-up on the last part of it." The soundman will tell you "not to drop the ends of your lines." And, finally, the costume guy will whisper, "Pssst . . . could you try not to let your shirt bunch up when you sit down." Meanwhile your every move is marked on the floor with tape by stage hands (who all, for some reason, look like out-of-work cowboys), and you will be expected to "hit those marks" exactly, every time.

Somewhere in all of this *you'll* be trying to do a little acting. But the priority of the people around you will be that you do what *they* need you to do, and do it right, because life on a film set is a game of inches, and time is money.

One of the most painful experiences I have ever seen was an actor who was hired to do one day's work on a TV show. During the filming of his scene, the poor guy kept messing up the one small piece of action he had—which happened to be pivotal to the story. The director and the crew were quite diplomatic about it, but it was clear that the actor was turning to toast before everyone's eyes. And no one knew it better than the actor himself.

I'm sure this actor had trained long and hard at his craft and knew how to interpret characters and play scenes and summon emotions. But, along the way, no one ever told him that all those noble efforts could unravel in public embarrassment if he was a klutz under pressure and couldn't be coordinated when he *had* to be.

Of course, some people are born with better coordination than others. I know people who never seem to botch anything and others who spill a glass of red wine at every occasion. (Why is it the spillers always like *red* wine?) Whether you are generally coordinated or not, you can (and should) always be working to improve your coordination as an actor.

Always demand pinpoint coordination from yourself *whenever* you act, whether it's at a rehearsal, in a scene for acting class, or even practicing for an audition in your living room. Make a conscious effort to do every action with precision. Don't accept "rehearsal sloppiness" from yourself. Think of it as practice for the day you may find yourself on a pressure-filled film set.

Be very strict with yourself about one of the big "coordination" pitfalls for actors, especially good actors. Sometimes the emotions in a big scene can turn an actor into a clumsy and *dangerous* mess. The scene heats up and things start flying.

Great emotion in a scene will be of no use if there are projectiles hurtling into frame. On the very first day of shooting *The Godfather*, the actress Talia Shire (Francis Ford Coppola's real-life sister), who played the role of Connie in the film, had a very emotional scene. She got so worked up that she slammed into the (very expensive) camera and knocked it over. No director will ever fire you for this—so long as you're his sister. Everyone else, watch out.

I know a brilliant actor who has a phenomenal emotional range. But whenever the scene heats up, you almost feel like the people he's acting with should be wearing safety goggles. Things go flying. He works some in theater but never in film or TV.

(This issue can also apply to theater acting. Face it, no matter how hot your emotions are in the nunnery scene from *Hamlet*, they will be lost on the audience if they see Ophelia get poked in the eye.)

The lines are probably the most difficult of all the elements that have to be coordinated. Exactitude of lines—getting them down *word for word*—is even more important in film than it is in theater. *For technical reasons.*

Because cuts and edits will be done to the timing of the words you speak, and because different *takes* of the same line may be used, you should say your lines using the same words every time and speak the dialogue cleanly. Clean dialogue means that you don't add in some of those little "sloppy extras" that have a way of working themselves into our speech.

One of the most common "sloppy extras" is to add a very faint "ya know" or "I mean" between the written lines. While we have become so used to these tics that we hardly notice them, they make the actor sound tentative and make the character lose depth as perceived by an audience.

Another sloppy extra that weakens the effect of a character is to launch the line by stuttering the first word, as in "It . . . It . . . It hurts me." Instead of "It hurts me." Sound men will hate you, directors will be miffed, and I find it's a vocal mannerism that weakens an actor.

## *In film, don't think about the words as you say them*

In an earlier note I discussed the need for theater actors to "shape" their performances. In film the reverse is true. There are many forces at work in a movie that do the shaping of your performance for you—things like camera angles and movements, editing and musical score. So if your performance seems as if you are *shaping* it, you'll come across as an "actor" and not the character. Bad screen actors seem to be "playing" the camera moves instead of ignoring them, or "playing" the incidental music rather than simply saying real words.

In its most common form this "overshaping" inhibits the way actors speak. Lines can sound like lines, spoken in a way that is overly formed, or deliberately musicalized, or given too much emphasis. All of which will sound false to the ear of the listener. Most people can tell the difference between someone who is saying "prepared" lines and someone who is making up the words on the spot. Even if a good actor is speaking the made-up words, if you listen closely you can still tell the difference.

Next time you are channel surfing, close your eyes and listen to different shows, trying to guess if the person you hear talking is "real" or acting a part. You'll be amazed how quickly you'll be able to tell if someone is saying "lines" (e.g., an actor doing a fictional show) or saying real, spontaneous words (e.g., the news, an interview). In a day and age when reality shows are filmed like dramas and dramas are filmed like reality shows, it still only takes a second for me to know whether the show is "real" or "fictional," simply by the way people speak.

Then try something else. Use that "Previous Channel" button on the remote and switch back and forth between the "real" person and the one who's acting to see if you can figure out the difference in how they "sound."

What you'll find is that the *real* person's voice is freer and less *presentational*. Real people just *speak*, making no attempt whatsoever to *do* anything with their voices. The actors' voices sound more consciously controlled, as if they are deliberately *putting* emotional colors into the sound of it.

The nonactor who's making up words on the spot can't do too much with his voice in the way of coloring it, because his brain isn't able to think about the words as they come out of his mouth. The brain is too busy composing the next set of words to send down to the mouth. In a manner of speaking, the brain is so busy "writing" it can't focus on the words that are being spoken as they come out of the mouth.

You'll be able to get this effect if you train yourself *never to think of the words as they are coming out of your mouth*. Think of anything else—even some random thought, unrelated to the scene—rather than think too much about the words as they flow from you in speech.

Pay attention to this the next time you act. You'll be amazed at how much of your focus will keep wanting to deal with the words as they come out of your mouth. It will not be easy to pull your brain away from being conscious of the words you're speaking, but keep trying. It will give you a much more realistic sound.

And *sound* never lies. W*ords* lie, but sound can't.

## *In film, beware of adrenaline acting*

When asked to describe the difference between theater acting and film acting, Al Pacino said, "I was used to working on a tightrope on stage. A movie is *just a line painted on the floor.*"

Theater *is* a tightrope, as is any situation in which you can't stop what you're doing to fix it, and can fail publicly. But it's this "danger" that makes theater acting *easier* than film acting in one significant way: in theater there is always *adrenaline* available. Everyone involved, from the actors to the usherettes, can feel that an important event is about to take place, and it makes the air tingle. Actors can draw on that adrenaline and use it to juice their work.

But film actors don't have this source of power available to them, because when you take away the audience and replace it with being able to start-over-if-you-flub, the adrenaline goes and the tightrope turns into a line painted on the floor. Furthermore the sort of amped-up energy common to theater is not welcome on film sets, where an atmosphere of relaxed efficiency is preferred. So film actors can't rely on any power source other than what they are able to muster up on their own.

Consequently many film actors come up with other kinds of acting stimuli for themselves. Some go to fairly daring extremes to do so. A lot of them start romances with the actors they play opposite. As cynical as this may sound, I think many of them do it as a way of generating an interesting energy that can be used to fuel their acting. Others try to fire themselves up by creating a sense of crisis about the project itself. They manufacture danger to the tune of: "I'll show this asshole director!" Or "Oh my God, I'll never be able to do this role, and it will ruin my career!"

Both these adrenaline replacements can work, though they come with inherent dangers. (But maybe that's the point.)

Another major source of fuel for a film actor—and perhaps the most common—is simply *making the project meaningful*. All actors use some degree of inspiration to spur their acting. But in my experience, great actors do more than use inspiration: they crave it, inhale it, devour it. Notice how many actors talk in interviews about how "meaningful" a project is to them, how much it matters, how profoundly it has changed them. They do every film with their whole soul, as if it were their last, because of how important it is to them. Even if the project isn't, they know they have to "fake it till they make it," so to speak. They need that meaning, that fuel of faith to light their work, even if they have to manufacture it.

## In film, the great actor changes himself or herself

Theater is the *arena*, a place where "fights" are staged. So on stage the tension should happen *between* actors. Film, however, is *pictures*, moving pictures. And the *greatest pictures are always of an individual with something interesting going on inside*.

That's why, in film, the tension should happen *within* the actor.

The most memorable scenes in film may take place "between" two people, but the image you *remember* is always the way a *moment of change* crosses the face of a good film actor. Think Jodie Foster listening to Hannibal Lecter, or Ingrid Bergman saying goodbye to Rick, or Charlie Chaplin holding a rose, his finger pressed to his lips.

You stand a chance of being a great film actor if you can show your audience what Yeats calls "the sorrows of your changing face." Not to have *the character* change, but for *you* the actor to change, from within, right before our eyes. You have to let the tension inside you battle itself out, and you must then let your audience see what this does in you. Because that's the picture that will stay with them.

One famous piece of film that shows the changing face of a great actor and a character consumed by the tension from within is in *The Godfather*. Al Pacino as Michael Corleone emerges from a bathroom with a concealed gun that he's about to use to kill two people with whom he's sitting in a restaurant. It will be the character's initiation into murder.

The tension Pacino plays while sitting at the table isn't between his character and the two people he's going to kill, the tension he plays is *within* him, between the innocent nonkiller that he is and the murderer he soon will be.

It's one of the most brilliantly tense scenes in any movie. In this scene we don't just see a character change; we see an *actor* change, a human being change. Indeed, when the studio executives who were planning to fire Pacino saw this scene, they recognized his genius for the first time and changed their minds.

Good film acting changes the actor. If you cannot yet go through enough of an emotional change, it means you have work to do.

But that's the wonderful thing about acting: it's always ready to teach you *what you cannot feel.* And to get a lesson like that every day at work makes it a damn fine job.

---

## Summary of Notes on Stage and Screen

1. *The difference is dimensional.*
2. *The difference isn't in how you do things but in what you choose to do.*
3. *In theater, stillness works like a close-up does on screen.*
4. *In theater, your performance needs to be shaped.*
5. *In theater, go beyond the text.*
6. *In theater, the great actor changes the room.*
7. *In film, try to avoid the "mask acting" of theater.*
8. *In film, the acting isn't smaller, it's closer.*
9. *In film, emotion shouldn't be ugly.*
10. *In film, stay within the script.*
11. *In film, you have to be coordinated.*
12. *In film, don't think about the words as you say them.*
13. *In film, beware of adrenaline acting.*
14. *In film, the great actor changes himself or herself.*

---

# EPILOGUE

---

# "Notes and hopes . . ."

---

*Here is a lovely new notebook to*
*fill full of notes*
*A lovely new notebook to fill*
*full of hopes,*
*And notes and hopes . . .*
—*Gertrude Stein to Alice B. Toklas*

I have always loved the idea of notes and the habit of putting things into note form. But during the writing of this book I was especially drawn to any comment I heard or read about notes or note-taking or notebooks. My favorite (and certainly the jolliest) is this quotation from Gertrude Stein. So I thought I'd close with it.

I particularly like that last phrase: "notes and hopes." To me, *notes* and *hopes* are interconnected ideas. Every *note* to an actor is *hopeful*, because it's rooted in the belief that a few important words can lead to that magic moment of acting that those who do it and love it are always looking for.

So there you have it: a book of notes and hopes. Everything I've always wanted to say to an actor shrunk into ninety-four brief notions. You will, I'm sure, add dozens more of your own along the way. Because that's what actors do.

They make notes and take notes. And they hope.

# INDEX

Abbott, George, 138, 139
*Ace Ventura* (film), 134
Acting: as bad, 13, 14; calling
attention to, 13, 15; and
chemistry, 34; clichés of,
100; and creative state, 10;
and emotion, 40, 41; and
exhaustion, 113; and
friendship, 114, 115; as
good, 14, 24, 63, 73; and
honesty, 10; and hyper-self-
consciousness, 12; as
indulgent, 17; love, as
technique, 49, 50, 51; and
mini-thoughts, 48; as
mysterious, 4; and nuance,
48; and one-dimensional
characterization, 100; and
physical actuality, 74, 75; as
powerful, 20; pretending,
ability to, 37, 38; process of
vs. result of, 19; and self-
image, 24, 25; types of, 7; as
untruthful, 15. *See also*

Actors; Bad acting; Good
acting; Great acting.
*Actor Prepares, An*
(Stanislavski), 74
Actors: acting methods,
identity with, 19; and
audiences, 15, 16, 17; and
auditions, 22, 23, 27, 28;
and awkwardness, 102,
103; as bad, 24, 73, 74, 79,
97, 98; blocks of, 107, 108;
and concentration, 46, 47;
and downtime, 26;
dramatic, as drawn to, 20,
21; egos of, 12; and
emotion, 102; and emotional
intelligence, 45; emotional
sensitivity in, 32; and
epiphanies, 4; failure,
processing of, 115; as good,
24, 63, 73, 80; as great,
goal of, 25; great vs. good,
6; and gutter-balls, 85, 86,
87; idea, as passionate

212 · *Index*

214 · *Index*

## A NOTE ON THE AUTHOR

Ron Marasco was born in Westwood, New Jersey, and after graduation from Fordham University studied at the Moscow Art Theatre and then at the University of California, Los Angeles, where he received a Ph.D. in theater. As an actor he has appeared on stage, in movies, and on television. He has also directed award-winning plays and has written screenplays. Mr. Marasco is professor of theater at Loyola Marymount University in Los Angeles. He lives in Playa Del Rey, California.